They Write Your Name on a Grain of Rice

LORI JAKIELA

Acknowledgments:
Parts of this collection have appeared, sometimes in different forms, in the following publications: *Belt Magazine, Hippocampus, Pulse: Voices from the Heart of Medicine, Full Grown People, Pittsburgh Magazine, Brevity Magazine, The Offing, KGB BarLit, Superstition Review, Fatal Flaw, The Pittsburgh Post-Gazette, The Washington Post, Chautauqua Magazine, Mayday Magazine, Pittsburgh Quarterly, Prometheus Dreaming, Drunk Monkeys.*

Thanks very much to the editors.

An Atticus Trade Paperback Original

12625 N Saguaro Blvd Ste 111
Fountain Hills, AZ 85268
http://atticusbooksonline.com

ISBN-13: 978-0-9915469-9-2

Interior design by David McNamara / Publish Publish
Cover design by Alban Fischer

Let's say we're seriously ill, need surgery—
which is to say we might not get up
from the white table.
Even though it's impossible not to feel sad
about going a little too soon,
we'll still laugh at the jokes being told,
we'll still look out the window to see if it's raining.

—Nazim Hikmet

"You must go on. I can't go on. I'll go on."

—Samuel Beckett

For Newman.

Beloved on this earth and whatever comes next.

Table of Contents

Author's Note: Elevator Pitch 1

Part 1

Prayer to the Patron Saint of Companionship 11
Hope Is the Thing with Feathers 17

Part 2

Soft 23
Holy 29
Family History of X 33
The Success Dream Book 37
God Damn It, Be Kind 59
With Great Power Comes Great Responsibility 73

Part 3

Say You Want to Live and Be Beautiful: A Memoir of a Diagnosis
Prologue 81
Chapter 1: Except for the Cancer, I'm Fine 83
Chapter 2: Lynyrd Skynyrd and the Expanding Universe of Vowels 99
Chapter 3: Jokes About Needles Probably Aren't Funny 111
Chapter 4: I See You, Beauty 121

Chapter 5: I Would Love to Write a Book Like a Stephen King Book 131
Chapter 6: Boring, Sidney 133
Chapter 7: Your One Phone Call 139
Chapter 8: In the Womancare Waiting Room, I Consider Flamingoes 153
Chapter 9: I Got You, Babe 159
Chapter 10: They Write Your Name on a Grain of Rice 165
Chapter 11: Proof of Life 171
Chapter 12: Adult Mart 189
Chapter 13: Andy Warhola Meets the Breatharians 195
Chapter 14: Go Beyond the Pain 203

Epilogue 1: Tommy Lee's Penis and Me 207
Epilogue 2 211

In Gratitude 213

About the Author 214

Elevator Pitch

Author's Note

Writers, like Hollywood people, are supposed to have an elevator pitch—a line you say in case you end up stuck in an elevator with your dream literary agent, or, better, Sean Penn, that rough angel, or Greta Gerwig, or Wes Anderson, or Jane Campion, an artist with money who wants to option your book.

My beautiful friend Senora fell four floors in a New York elevator once. It took her many years with specialists and a chiropractor to get her spine steady again.

When I was a flight attendant, an airplane dropped 10,000 feet in seconds and I was thrown a few rows. My beautiful Senora gave me the name of her chiropractor. He was a tiny man who climbed my back like a spider monkey. He worked my spine until all the bones clicked in place like Scrabble tiles.

I love Scrabble. I love *Words with Friends*. I love words, though their power is limited, I know.

"To me, the greatest pleasure of writing is not what it's about, but the music the words make," Truman Capote said.

I love Truman Capote's writing. *Breakfast at Tiffany's. Other Voices, Other Rooms.* Truman Capote wrote America's first nonfiction novel, *In Cold Blood.* He hung out with Andy Warhol, who will show up in this book again and again.

Truman Capote died of liver disease, plus an overdose of pills and a fatal infusion of writer-guilt at the home of Joanna Carson, talk-show host Johnny Carson's fourth wife. Truman was 59 years old, just a little older than I am now. Truman Capote said he didn't care what anyone said about him so long as it wasn't true.

Because he needed an ending for *In Cold Blood,* Truman Capote left a murderer, who thought Truman was a friend, to die alone on death row. Truman Capote was a jealous jerk to his friend, Harper Lee, who once defended him from bullies on a playground when they were children. No one in Holcomb, Kansas would have talked to Truman Capote, with his cashmere scarf and Mike-Tyson-as-debutante voice, if it weren't for Harper Lee.

Read *To Kill a Mockingbird* if you didn't in high school. It's genius.

Read *In Cold Blood.* It's genius.

If you'd like, we can talk about the cost of all of this, the weight of all those words, that music. Over wine, maybe. Coffee, if you're trying to do better.

Andy Warhola, with the "a," was from Pittsburgh, Pennsylvania. He dropped the "a" when he moved to New York and denied his roots.

In the 1970s, Andy Warhol traded a portrait of Truman Capote to Truman Capote in exchange for a year's worth of Truman Capote columns for *Interview* magazine.

Fuck you, Andy Warhola.

Most writers need cash-money for their work. Maybe not Truman, but still.

Andy Warhol/a was a great artist but a questionable human. Truman Capote was a brilliant writer but a questionable human.

"Home is where you feel at home," Truman Capote said. "I'm still looking."

Truman Capote, born in New Orleans, raised in Alabama and so forth, was cremated. Some of his remains are buried in Los Angeles. Some were mixed with his partner Jack Dunphy's remains and scattered in Long Island, New York. Another portion was auctioned off in 2016 and sold to an anonymous buyer for $43,750.

"Love, having no geography, knows no boundaries."

Truman Capote said that, too.

Andy Warhol said he wanted to be a robot. One of his favorite things to say was, "So what."

Bless you, Truman. Bless you, Andy.

Bless you, Senora, my dear friend. I hope you're well and pain-free and summering in the Hamptons with no elevator in sight.

Bless you, tiny chiropractor, patron saint of spines. I'm sorry I've forgotten your name.

Dear reader:

I hope you'll find some music in this book.

Maybe that's an elevator pitch.

In the building I lived in during my years in New York, the super, Jay, who wanted to be called Jay-Z, who no one called Jay-Z, told me all elevator inspections were faked, just like the pesticides he supposedly sprayed to kill cockroaches. Pesticides were, apparently, expensive. Water wasn't.

"We give them a nice shower," Jay said about the roaches, who didn't seem to mind the spritz.

Fun fact: Cockroaches love toothpaste. If you live in New York, remember to keep your toothbrush in the refrigerator—one of the few places roaches won't look for snacks.

Keep your cereal in there, too.

About elevators.

My friend Senora took the stairs a lot.

I took the stairs a lot.

I take the stairs a lot.

In the building I lived in, my friend Moose, who I loved even though he did time in and out of jail, "three hots and a cot," was legendary for once dangling a guy over an elevator shaft.

The guy owed some people money. Moose worked for those people the guy owed money to.

"I wouldn't never drop nobody on purpose," Moose, my otherwise gentle friend, said.

The guy Moose dangled was fine, I think.

Bless you, Moose.

Bless you, guy who Moose dangled.

May all our debts be paid, amen.

An elevator pitch is a sentence that says what a book, which is kind of an elevator stuffed full of words, is about.

This book you're kind enough to hold—thank you—is a meandering, spiraling map of sorts, a time-capsule of an ordinary life as it builds to a cancer diagnosis, the aftermath of that.

That is the worst elevator pitch in the history of elevator pitches.

Sorry, Sean Penn. Sorry Greta Gerwig, you genius.

Sorry, everyone.

Andy Warhol has a series he called *Time Capsules*–cardboard boxes filled with scraps of his everyday life. There are over 600 Warhol capsules. Critics call the capsules archival goldmines.

Time Capsule 21 includes a Dick Tracy detective novel, a collection of pink While You Were Out notes, a cartoon cat that says "hello," and a picture of a shoe.

"So what," Andy Warhol would say.

What you're about to read—thank you again—is a map of mortality, of a mind distracted by everyday things like cancer and breasts, airplanes and emotional-support animals, family and loss, EPA clean-up zones, tender humans, flawed writers and artists, lost bedazzled turtles and homing pigeons, and the many ways we're all connected.

"The idea is not to live forever," Andy Warhol said. "It is to create something that will."

Andy's Campbell's Soup cans are magnets on my fridge. They hold grocery lists and bills. They hold to-do lists and checks that need to be cashed and news clippings.

They anchor pictures of my children, my heart.

My fridge is a map of my life, maybe. Yours probably is a map of your life, too. Take a look. I'll wait.

Back when people had to use maps, I got lost constantly. My sense of direction takes me left when I should go right, and once in a while I veer purposely off-course, like that time I was headed to Ohio but figured New York City was just a bit further down the road. Or that time I was headed to Harrisburg but figured that was halfway to New York City.

Or that time I was in Philly and figured just one more bridge. Or that time I was in New Jersey and there was just a tunnel between us.

God how I miss New York, a lover I need to see just one more time to be sure it won't work out.

How I love Pittsburgh, my steady home country, too.

No matter how much Andy Warhol believed in his New York-ness, the Andy Warhol Museum is here in Pittsburgh. I should mention that.

No matter how many years I lived in New York, Moose called me "Pittsburgh."

"Hey Pittsburgh," he'd say. "What you got for me?"

I'd bring Moose chocolates I'd buy overseas. He wasn't supposed to have them, methadone, etc., but Moose loved chocolate, and our time with one another is so short.

Everyone should have as much sweetness as possible in this life.

This is a book about that, too.

"I'll say a prayer for you, Pittsburgh," Moose would say and throw up a gang sign.

"Yo, Pittsburgh," Moose would say and give me the finger, but sweet like.

I love this world. Don't you?

Tell me everything you love. I'll mark it here.

"I think it would be very glamorous to be reincarnated," Andy Warhol said, "as a great big ring on Liz Taylor's finger."

In her lifetime, the rings on Elizabeth Taylor's fingers included the 33-carat Krupp diamond, the 69.42-carat Taylor-Burton, and the 50-carat La Peregrina Pearl. When Elizabeth Taylor died, her jewelry sold for $156.8 million dollars at auction, with all the money going to support AIDS research to help others live.

Elizabeth Taylor's funeral started 15 minutes late, in accordance with her final wish—to be late to her own funeral.

Elizabeth Taylor's eyes were violet.

Imagine.

Elevator pitch:

Even our darkness is lit with glitter and shine.

Part 1

Prayer to the Patron Saint of Companionship

"Why would you bring a child into this world?" people liked to ask back in the 1900s. Why would anyone ask such a thing?

"Hope is the thing with feathers –
that perches in the soul-
and sings the tune without the words –
and never stops — at all —"

That's Emily Dickinson.

Emily Dickinson never had children. Emily Dickinson wrote beautiful poems, which are their own legacy.

I once misread that poem, and via some brain slip, inserted the world *coul* for soul. I am, by title at least, a writer and college professor, so I spent hours looking up the word *coul*. It means a few things.

In this case I thought Dickinson might have meant a chimney cover, though *coul* is also a term in fencing, as in swords.

Forget swords. For a flammable-feathered bird to perch in a chimney and risk flames is hope enough.

Some days I believe my version more than Emily's.

Birdbrain, people say, meaning stupid, but birds are some of the smartest animals on the planet. Ravens and crows are great at holding grudges, second only to humans.

Don't fuck with crows. They remember your face.

For seven years, I worked as a flight attendant for a major airline, where I learned a little about human/animal traits.

Did you know birds are designated support animals? But some birds and animals are more designated and acceptable than others.

Most airlines are cool with cockatoos. Most airlines are flexible with parrots because parrots talk back, which makes them seem more like human passengers, though most flight attendants dream of human passengers who don't talk back unless those passengers have some kindness to give.

Be nice to your flight crew. Please and thank you.

Not too long ago, United Airlines denied boarding to Brooklyn artist Ventiko who wanted to travel with her emotional support peacock, Dexter. Dexter hated the subway but was cool with planes. Ventiko put Dexter on a baggage trolley, where other passengers could admire him. Ventiko offered to put Dexter through the X-ray scanner, because no peacock had ever been identified as a terrorist or a weapon. Ventiko offered to buy Dexter his own seat on the plane, but United declined.

Have you ever heard a peacock scream? It's impressive. It goes on for days. The echo of that wouldn't do well in the test-tube of an airplane cabin.

Ventiko and Dexter eventually opted to drive, *On the Road* style, for the betterment of all.

"Peacocks represent infinity and immortality," Ventiko told the *LA Times*, explaining Dexter's mass appeal.

Ventiko kept a log of their journeys and Dexter ended up with more than 17,000 followers on Instagram. Ventiko painted Dexter many times. He shows up in her work as Santo Dexter, Patron Saint of Companionship.

There are so many other airlines vs. animal stories:

Gizmo the marmoset—86'd for pooping on board;

Daniel Turducken Stinkerbutt, a duck—beloved on his American Airlines' flight;

Coco the bunny—earned a coveted upgrade to Business Class for his classy bowtie;

Daisy the Squirrel—denied boarding because squirrel.

But the saddest and most interesting to me is Pebbles the hamster, who died an untimely death when her owner, a college student, tried to board a Spirit Airlines flight with Pebbles as her companion. The student was trying to get home to deal with a medical issue. Later she said someone from the airline told her she had two choices—set Pebbles free or flush him down the toilet.

No airline person I know, and I flew for seven years, would ever suggest killing an animal, though they may think of creative ways to hurt humans from time to time. Coffee spills in turbulence. Red wine spills in turbulence. Visine in coffee (don't ask). And so on.

After trying for hours to find another way home, the student flushed Pebbles and got on the plane.

Spirit Airlines has denied ever offering the toilet option.

If your support animal is your support animal, how do you flush it? How does anyone let go of the things that tether them to this life?

RIP, Pebbles.

\ı /

One time when I was still flying, a man tried to smuggle his Chihuahua on board.

TSA agents boarded the flight just before takeoff. "Excuse me, sir," one TSA agent, a loaf of white bread in a tight red blazer, said. "We know you have a dog in your pocket."

The man, 38B, wore a leather jacket, zipped tight. This was July in Orlando, Florida.

Florida, the punchline of so many jokes. Florida man, Florida man. Florida, the birthplace of Dexter the peacock. Florida, the place everyone I knew back home in Pittsburgh thought of as heaven—the place to go to retire, the place to go to die.

38B said, "What?"

He said, "I have no idea what you're talking about," and fiddled with his jacket zipper.

My parents built a house in Florida, but had to sell it when my mother got sick. In the battle between dreams and mortality, mortality always wins.

"Some goddamn joke," my father said back then. "A real kick in the ass."

The house was lovely—pink stucco, across the street from a canal filled with flying fish that seemed to leap from fairytales.

I remember shopping for furniture to fill the house. I remember buying silverware, extra sets of knives and forks and soup spoons, though who eats soup in Florida? I remember lizards who'd latch onto the screen doors, their green skin glistening, their tails coiled into question marks, their long nails like fishhooks holding on.

I remember my parents fighting. Always that.

I thought if they could have just made it to Florida to live, they'd stop fighting. I thought if they just made it to Florida, they'd live.

Florida's official state slogan is, "In God We Trust."

The unofficial slogans: "The Sunshine State," "God's Waiting Room," "America's Wang."

"We know," the TSA agent on the plane said, and jerked a thumb toward 38B's jacket.

"We should have known," my father said, meaning the world wasn't a place designed for him and people like him and my mother to dream Florida dreams or have access to lives they weren't born into.

"A place for everyone and everyone in their place," my mother, who loved to mix metaphors and clichés, used to say.

"We saw the skeleton, sir," the TSA agent on the plane said.

38B, in a moment of pure Florida-man-inspired genius and hope, had tucked his tiny dog into his leather jacket and sent it through the X-ray machine, figuring his jacket—thick, squeaky, probably not real leather at all—would block it some.

The Chihuahua, when 38B pulled it out, wriggled and squeaked. It was tiny, just a puppy.

38B looked guilty, apologetic, then just sad.

The TSA agent escorted 38B and his tiny dog off the flight and I felt bad about everything.

Having a support animal on board is expensive. Not everyone who needs a little help can afford the luxury. Some dreams are so small they seem within reach, even when they're not.

The dog could fit in the palm of my hand. He wouldn't have hurt anything.

Maybe my parents would have been happy in Florida.

Maybe they would be alive, even now.

As for birds, sorry Dexter.

I've seen Hitchcock.

Those birds knew exactly what they were doing.

There are a lot of birds in Emily Dickinson's poems, but even more Death.

Living with Death as a roommate in your brain may have made the thought of children unbearable to anyone, but even Emily Dickinson got lonely and adopted a dog. She named her dog Carlo and called him Baby.

Carlo lived for 16 years. Dickinson, that lover of death, was by all accounts devastated when Carlo died.

I love animals. The loss of anything and anyone we love is an aberration.

There is no such thing as a good death.

Hope Is the Thing with Feathers

When my son Locklin was a month old, he became very sick. He started throwing up and kept throwing up and ended up in the hospital.

The hospital ID band on my son's wrist fit on my ring finger. I could cradle my son's whole body in my hands.

The oxygen meter clamped to his finger was the size of a paper clip. It glowed red and blue, the colors of emergency, tiny police lights flashing against bleached hospital sheets.

Helpless, terrified, I sat by my son's hospital bed for three nights, pumping milk from breasts he was too sick to suck while a nurse kept bringing me food I couldn't eat.

My husband was working long hours then, with a power-suit-wearing boss who said a sick kid was no reason to take time off.

"Oh, please," the boss said. "Your wife can handle it."

I was trying.

"You have to try," the nurse who brought my meal trays said. "You need to eat to keep the milk coming for when he's better."

The nurse was lovely.

Most nurses are lovely, but some more so.

This nurse, whose name I don't remember, such is the mind under stress, wore a smock with Elmo and Big Bird all over it. Her lips were pink satin. She wore designer clogs painted with cardiograms, the visual rendering of healthy, beating hearts.

She brought me cartons of milk. She brought me hospital brownies. She brought me saltines and tea and grilled cheese sandwiches. She brought me Jell-O, that hospital staple that still makes me gag.

As a child, I spent so much time in hospitals. Born with badly clubbed feet, I had many surgeries.

My first memories are of hospitals—the squeak of nurses' white shoes on linoleum, the clang of bed pans and call bells, the icy press of stethoscopes on bare skin, the way the squeeze of blood-pressure cuffs made, still makes, me nauseous.

Once, when I was in traction, a nurse's aide left a tray of green Jell-O for me to eat. She laid the tray across my stomach. Both of my legs were suspended mid-air. My head was supposed to stay flat on the pillow. There are many things impossible to eat when in this position, but Jell-O might be the most impossible.

"You have to eat," the nurses said back then, not unkindly, and I tried. I wanted to be a good patient, the best patient. My mother was a nurse and I wanted to make her proud. I wanted to not be an embarrassment. But the Jell-O seemed alive. It squirmed off my spoon and plopped onto the white sheets, the way frogs sometimes fell from the sky in the Bible and my parents' beloved Florida.

I'm thinking of this now, though I haven't been to Florida in years.

Frogs sometimes filled up ice bins at the Florida motels my parents could afford on vacation back in the 1970s and '80s. The frogs skittered around the edges of motel pools. They were everywhere, a plague, but a cute one—their big eyes, those splayed feet clinging to every tree and lamp post.

"Paradise," my Pittsburgh people call Florida.

"You have to eat," the lovely nurse caring for my son said.

She said, "Please."

She said, "Try, Mom."

When you're a mother, everyone in the medical establishment calls you Mom. Your name, whatever that meant once, is over. Whoever you thought you were is finished. The body you thought was yours becomes not yours.

At first, I was angry about it. Then I was grateful.

There is nothing more honest. Nothing in my life has ever felt more honest.

My son looked so fragile in his bed, with the hospital rails pulled up on both sides like a jail cell.

I slid one hand through the bars and kept it on his chest to feel his breathing. I watched the oxygen meter flash blue for oxygen, red for blood.

I've read that blue and red are designated for emergencies because everyone can recognize those two colors, even the colorblind. People who are colorblind to red can see blue, vice-versa. Anyone looking at the tiny body of my son in that bed could see this emergency for what it was. Everything around us smelled urgent—alcohol swabs and bleach and metal, sweat and breast milk. My job as Mom was to watch and wait. Check the colors. Make sure my son kept breathing. Suction his nose and mouth. Keep his airway clear.

"Please, Mom," the lovely nurse said.

My job was to pump and keep pumping my breasts, which leaked and hurt and swelled. I expressed the milk. God, that word, expressed–*to convey a thought or feeling, to squeeze out.*

The milk leaked then sprayed, pale blue-ish white, the color of oysters, cataracts, thin as rain, sugar water, into tiny bottles the nurse gave me. I labeled them with my son's name just in case he could keep anything down.

The nurse took the bottles like offerings back to a refrigerator filled with other bottles labeled with the names of other mothers' children.

So many children were sick that year. There was a virus. There is often a virus, but once you have a child that word becomes more terrifying. The hospital hallways echoed with the sound of crying and the air felt heavy, as if worry had the power to shift gravity.

I think it does.

In Florida, those frogs seemed like a miracle or a curse, both maybe.

Sometimes I can still see my mother's lovely, worried face, the way it seemed to hover above my childhood hospital bed as I drifted like an astronaut in and out of drugged sleep.

"Please, Mom."

The disease my son had, respiratory syncytial virus or RSV, is so common nearly all children get it by the time they are two years old. I didn't know that then. I didn't know anything about parenting, or the terror and joy that come with it. I'm still learning.

My son is twenty-one years old now, beautiful, healthy. Sometimes he falls asleep on the couch after work, and I'll drape a blanket over him, then take a minute.

Express a thought or feeling.

Still here.

Still here.

Part 2

Soft

My daughter Phelan weeps every New Year's Eve. It started when she was four years old. Decked out in party hats that cut lines into our cheeks, we watched Anderson Cooper and Kathy Griffin pretend-flirt as the ball started to fall like a small planet over Times Square.

Phelan leaned into me and her body stiffened like she was bracing for impact. When everyone yelled "Happy New Year!" and fireworks and confetti filled the TV screen, Phelan buried her face in my hair. She flung herself at her father's chest and swatted her brother Locklin. She dropped to the floor, boneless, inconsolable.

"Goodbye, goodbye," she cried, as the TV blared Sinatra. *If I can make it there.*

"I miss the good old days," Phelan said later, and I said, "You're four, sweetie."

My daughter was born with a beautiful sense of nostalgia.

"Old soul," my friend Tonya says.

Tonya runs a yoga studio filled with Buddha statues and incense, dried flowers, and velvety drapes in our rusty mill town of Trafford. The studio used to be Mel's Barber Shop. The Westmoreland Ghost Hunters occasionally stop by, believing Mel, who played stand-up bass, haunts the place. When Tonya's alone at night, she hears music. She smells Barbasol.

Tonya knows old souls. I think she, like my daughter, is one.

When we replaced the floor in our kitchen, Phelan, who was seven, wept over that, too. She threw herself onto the sticky yellowed tiles that had been in place since the 1970s.

"Goodbye, floor," she said, like she was losing a friend.

I tried to pick her up, but again she went boneless, a gift some children have that allows them to turn their solid bodies viscous. Think *The Blob.* Think quicksand and lava.

Phelan wailed and pressed her face to the floor, which was not only old, but gross. Desiccated Cheerios, bits of old toast and cookie crumbs stuck in her long blonde curls.

I said, "Sweetheart, what's wrong? You'll love the new floor. You can slide across it in your socks. It'll be like ice skating."

"Really?" she said and tried to smile.

Then she went on weeping.

The same thing happened when we tried to replace the stained carpet in her bedroom, when we tried to paint her bedroom walls, and when our minivan died.

Phelan was eight when we bought a lime-green replacement Kia.

"Goodbye, van," she said. "We had some good times."

We let Phelan pick the car's color, thinking that might help with the weeping. Lime green was her favorite color that year. It showed up in every picture she drew. For a 100-days-of-school assignment, Phelan drew her 100-year-old self, what she imagined she'd be like as an old lady. She drew herself dancing, a stick figure full of joy, lime green jelly- bean feet, lime green curls, a lime green smile bigger than her sweetly squiggled head.

Green, the color of my daughter's eyes and my eyes and my son's eyes. Green, the color of Spring and hope, the color of money, the color of go.

"Your brother threw up in that van all the time," I said to diffuse things.

The car salesman, rubbing his comb-over, tried to console my daughter. He gave her a lollipop. He gave her a green balloon. Phelan thanked him and kept crying.

"What is wrong with that kid?" another salesman said.

"Why'd you let her pick that color?" Locklin said.

For the nearly ten years we had that car, my son called it the Booger Mobile and blamed it for any gap in his dating life.

When I was a child, I cried a lot. My mother, annoyed, worried, bought a book called *Cry-Baby Duck* and read it to me at bedtime.

Children's books have morals, and this one wanted kids to toughen up.

"Cry-baby duck," my mother would say whenever I was upset. "Let's have a pity party, one two three, awwww." She'd make a tiny violin with her fingers to play along.

The duck in that story cried because he wanted to be bigger, prettier, less duck-ish. The duck in that story cried whenever he didn't get his way. The duck in the story cried because he didn't fit. None of these were the reasons I cried, and my mother knew that.

"You and your feelings," she said, like feelings made her itchy, like feelings were something I, her adopted daughter, had been born with, a genetic flaw that needed to be fixed. "Grow a thicker skin already."

A few years ago, Phelan and I found a copy of *Cry-Baby Duck* and read it together. When we were done, my daughter looked stunned.

"What kind of monster reads a book like that to a child?" she said.

I didn't tell Phelan other things my mother would say, like "I'll give you something to cry about," or "Wait until you've lived long enough to have something to cry about."

I didn't tell my daughter about my mother's unhappiness, or my own, or how, in this life, happiness is something to cling to, a life raft.

When I look into my daughter's lovely eyes and see a reflection of my own, it feels like a miracle, a bit of magic. Nature, nurture, none of that matters much.

Whenever you feel it—magic, happiness—hold on.

Sometimes I worry my daughter is too sensitive. Sometimes I wish I could find armor to protect her from the loss that will come and keep coming.

My mother was no monster. She wasn't being cruel. She was afraid. Sometimes, I know now, mothers talking to their daughters are talking to themselves.

When I worry about Phelan, I try to remember that her capacity for tears is matched only by her capacity for joy.

One day, years ago, her brother caught her spinning and dancing in the kitchen.

"Life isn't all daisies and roses, you know," Locklin said.

Phelan kept spinning.

She laughed and said, "Who's Daisy?"

My daughter's first word was "abre," Spanish for "open." When she said it, she held her arms wide, reaching out of her crib, like she wanted to take everyone and everything in.

It could have been the influence of *Dora the Explorer*, which we watched over and over on videos and TV. It could have been because I liked to speak Spanish to my children, my small attempt to show them the beauty and vastness of the world. My Spanish is terrible and basic, New York-street Spanish mostly, but I love it so, the music of other worlds, the way it opens my heart, the way struggling with words reminds me of being a child, the joy of finding language for the experience of being alive. *Express.*

"Be soft," Kurt Vonnegut Jr. said. "Do not let the world make you hard."

My daughter is 17 now. Sometimes her big feelings embarrass her, I think. Life feels harder and crueler every day. Just turn on the news. Open your phone. And still.

A while back, Phelan and I visited Times Square, a place we both wanted her to see. She looked up at the Toshiba tower, the New Years' ball snuggled safely in place. Phelan looked around, the lights on Broadway, the smiling people taking pictures, the Naked Cowboy playing his guitar in his underwear.

"It's all too beautiful," she said about New York, about this life, about the world.

Holy

My mother worries about my soul. She tells me so at her kitchen table, 6 in the morning. We're making nutroll, even though it's not a holiday, nothing to celebrate.

My mother believes bread rises only in the morning. I'm not good with mornings. Last night I stayed up late, reading, worrying.

"Ruining your eyes," my mother says.

Drinking. I'm hungover. My mother is dying. From cancer. From her heart. Everything is urgent now.

My mother wants me to know things, like where she keeps the silver, how to shut off the water, how to make a decent nutroll.

"Who will teach you when I'm dead?" she says and pounds the dough so hard her strength makes death seem impossible.

This morning my mother wants to talk religion, something I've refused to do with her for years. She brushes flour off her velour pantsuit. She punches the dough like it's a face, mine.

She says, "You can't believe in nothing."

She says, "If you don't believe in anything, what is there?"

She says, "You idiot."

I clutch the coffee she's made, instant, too much cream and sugar, the way my father liked it, not me. He's been dead five years. I sit in his chair. The mug I'm holding was his, Batman, the image faded from his calloused hands. My mother's mug, full of lemon tea, is Robin, faded to a mask and cape and the word "Holy!"

My mother would kiss my father's bald, chemo'd head.

She'd say, "The dynamic duo."

"First one goes, then the other," the funeral director said.

\ı/

My dying mother wants to talk about God and faith over a pastry I'll never master no matter how important it is for her to hand this down.

A good daughter would say the words.

A good daughter would ease things.

"It's private," I say about my beliefs.

My mother says, "I changed your diapers, and now you want to talk about private."

She works the rolling pin like a threat. It was my grandmother's, then my mother's. Now it will come to me. The wood is worn to a honeyed shine, maple, like the trees my mother and I planted in the yard when I was a child.

My mother rolls the dough in a circle thin enough to see through, a lens to another dimension where she's still young, a Kool cigarette between her pink-tipped fingers, smoke rings rising from her lips, messages to decode.

The skin on my mother's hands is thin enough to see through, a lens to bone.

"I can't," I say about rolling dough that thin.

"Patience, jackass, patience," my mother says.

/ı\

"You'll go to hell," my mother says. "You know that."

On the table rests a blue prayer book, a tiny paperback my father carried in his pocket when he was sick, *Daily Devotions*, a Jesus fish in a circle on the cover.

The fish is drawn in one line—no beginning, no end.

My mother doles out ground nuts and sugar, cinnamon, warm milk, four spoonfuls to make the sign of the cross. I spread the mixture evenly, as thin as the dough, thinner, out to the edges because it's expensive and needs to last.

Once, at a wedding, my mother brought nutroll for the cookie table. Someone else brought nutroll too, but it wasn't pretty, the layers and dough too thick.

"What kind of asshole brings a nutroll like that?" my mother said, then put her perfect nutrolls on a tray.

She carried them table to table to be sure people knew which ones were hers.

All my life, I've loved my mother. All my life, I've disappointed her.

I'm not the daughter I want to be.

I'm not the daughter my mother wants.

"You have to believe, or you'll burn," my mother is saying.

The nut roll spreads between us, a black hole, a universe pocked with stars.

Once I got stoned with a scientist who tried to explain Einstein's theory of time and space. He held up a Taco Bell burrito he'd split in two. He showed me the layers.

He said time was like that, a tortilla folded in on itself, now and not now, forever.

"Time is not a clock and we are not second hands," he said, and bit into the burrito.

Diablo Sauce ran down his chin and caught in his Freudian beard.

I hate movies about time travel, though writing is always that. All those worlds and lives shaken up and spilled on a page, like dice, like Yahtzee, maybe, my mother's favorite.

I've forgotten how to play.

All I remember is yelling "Yahtzee," which meant winning, which meant we're done here, which meant Boom.

"It's all a horrible day-mare," Robin once said to Batman.

About the nutroll my mother and I made: it turned out okay.

It's been 18 years since my mother died.

She said, "You have to try to believe."

She said, "Do it for me."

She said, "Where will you be when I'm gone?"

Family History of X

When I am diagnosed with my own cancer, Dr. Johnson, who looks like the comedian Norm MacDonald and tells smart-ass jokes and likes to draw stick-figure breasts on a white board to show surgical options, will ask, "Do you have a family history of breast cancer?"

Dr. Johnson will have already drawn a series of disembodied breasts before he asks this. The breasts will be squared off, Lego nipples, nothing Victoria's Secret-ish, nothing human.

Years later, a high school principal in Florida will be fired for showing pictures of Michelangelo's "David" to students, such is the stupidity of humans when faced with the reality of human bodies, all that fragile beauty and terror.

But this is before that, even.

Forgive me.

Before my diagnosis, I will have been warned about Dr. Johnson's passion for sketching. When I call to make an appointment, Dr. Johnson's assistant will say, "Doc likes to draw a lot."

I will have no idea what she means, so I'll say, "Okay?"

I will say "okay" a lot. When another doctor shows me what she sees on my mammogram, snow flurries in my left breast, when she calls this *concerning*, a word neutral as oatmeal, I will say, "Okay."

When a nurse calls later, when she says, *I'm sorry*, when she says again *sorry sorry*, I will say, "Okay."

I will thank her.

I hope I will.

"Manners," the mother who raised and loved and worried over me said. "Whatever day you're having, put a smile on your goddamned face. Your problems are not other people's problems. Remember that."

My mother, the nurse. She was tough and lovely and she died. Breast cancer.

I am adopted. My mother's story is not my story.

"Where will you be when I'm gone?" my mother wanted to know and I would say here, for now.

Critics believe Andy Warhol's time capsules were a way for him to trick death. His capsules include toenail clippings, taxi receipts, one half-eaten sandwich.

"I was here, you know. I was," Amy Krause Rosenthal would say about why she wrote down the lovely minutiae of her life.

About my family history, I will tell Dr. Johnson, "I don't know," and Dr. Johnson will hold his Sharpie in mid-air and say, "Explain."

In another world, Dr. Johnson may be a great artist. Home with his wife, who he calls Mrs. Johnson, as in "Mrs. Johnson requires my presence at a gala and so I'm not scheduling surgeries then because I fear death," Dr. Johnson may paint masterpieces. He may paint happy little trees. But in his office, with his pocket full of Sharpies, he is forever limited.

I am limited, too.

When asked for my medical history, I always bumble. Adopted people don't often know their medical histories. It's something we must articulate on forms again and again. It makes me feel guilty, illegitimate, dirty.

Explain.

How can a person not have the answer to the most basic human questions?

History of cancer? Unknown.

History of heart disease? Unknown.

History of, history of, history of—unknown, unknown.

Explain. Explain.

"Being adopted is like a book with its first chapter torn out," author Jeannette Winterson says.

After my parents died, I did an adoption search. My daughter was born with a birth defect I'd had. I panicked. I hadn't thought much about genetics, what I might have handed down without knowing.

I'd been adopted through Catholic Charities. My Catholic Charities social worker held my thick, redacted file when we met, though she couldn't let me see it. My file was so ordinary—a worn manila folder, a case number scribbled on the tab.

The social worker said, "Sometimes these things work out, like on Oprah. Sometimes they don't."

She pushed my file across her desk, just out of reach.

"Most times," she said, "they don't."

The short version: I found my birth mother. I asked for a medical history. "For my daughter," I said, which was true and not true.

I wanted my birth mother to care a little. I wanted her to love me, even. Or love me enough to let me know if something in the genes she handed down would kill me. I wanted her to give me answers I could pass to my doctors so I wouldn't seem crazy or lost.

My birth mother refused to give me a medical history.

Instead, she wished me dead.

"I'm adopted," I will tell Dr. Johnson, who will say, "Ah!" and order genetic testing, which the insurance company will cover, considering.

Dr. Johnson will sketch a single mastectomy. Double mastectomy. Lumpectomy with chemo and radiation and so on. He will draw an image, then strike an X through it, and move on to the next, and the next. X. X. X.

What I know about the first chapters of my life—X.

What I know about my birth mother—X.

What I know about what my daughter might face—no genetic predisposition for breast cancer. My cancer—likely environmental.

Still.

X. X.

Spoiler alert: I will decide upon a double mastectomy.

"Don't heal your pain. Amputate."

That's advice I'd gotten years before from a poet. She wanted to teach me to write what was true and not settle for easy conclusions.

When Dr. Johnson sees my husband in the waiting room before my surgery, my husband will be reading a book of poems.

"You're going to need a bigger book," Dr. Johnson will say and wink.

My surgery will last 13 hours. It will be the best sleep I've had in years.

"When I go into surgery, I am completely Zen," a friend who has had many cancer surgeries says. "I feel peaceful. I feel fully myself."

One of my poet-teachers, Linda Pastan, wrote, "There is an age when you are most yourself."

The double mastectomy I will opt for will include DIEP reconstruction. Dr. Johnson will take away the cancer. My plastic surgeon, Dr. Gimbel, an elegant man whose staff will look like they came from the set of *Scrubs*, each one more beautiful than the next, will rebuild my breasts with fat he will suction from my belly and hips.

Not everyone can have this surgery. You need just the right amount of fat in just the right spots. I was, am chubby, curvy—a good specimen. Genetics. Whatever.

Before my surgery, I will have to stand against a wall and be photographed naked from the waist up.

"Don't worry, these won't show up on Facebook," Dr. Gimbel will say.

He will have some trouble with his camera. The photos will take longer than expected. I will stand there, exposed. I will turn right. Turn left.

"It's all from the neck down," Dr. Gimbel will say to comfort me.

My body, disembodied.

No head, no face, nothing to connect it to me at all.

The Success Dream Book

My father said many things that embarrassed me growing up. Most of these things he'd say loud, on repeat. Most of these things included the word "ass," which my father molded like play-dough into a fun factory of insults.

"Little Miss College," he'd say. "I have more brains in my ass than you have in

your head."

"Little Miss College," he'd say. "I could wipe my ass with what you know about love."

There were some standbys: "You can't tell your ass from a hole in the ground" and "You couldn't find your ass with both hands" and "Your ass thinks your shit don't stink. Trust me. It does."

Sometimes my father would revert to something simple like "dumbass," and I'd almost be disappointed, like he wasn't even trying.

None of this bothered me much. My father, the steelworker, was gruff, but he loved me, and I loved him back. The one thing he'd say, the one that cut, was this: "Wake up and face reality, you're living in a dream world, kid."

My father, I knew, had stopped living in a dream world years ago. He gave up singing. He gave up dancing. He gave up nice suits and cigars and, if he allowed himself a tiny sweetness—a lunchbox pie, a knock-off Twinkie—he ate it standing up in the corner of the kitchen, his back hunched with guilt at allowing himself this small pleasure.

I'd seen what all this giving up had done to him—every unhappiness etched on my father's face like a relief map.

"Don't be like me, kid."

My father said that, too.

When my father was dying, I tried to hold onto my dreams—flying, travel, New York, rootlessness—for as long as I could, even though I knew we all eventually wake up whether we want to or not.

One weekend, I was on a Stockholm trip, a 48-hour layover, when my mother called my hotel room to tell me my father, who'd been in remission, was once again very sick.

"He's talking in his sleep, in Polish," my mother said. "He's not right."

My mother, the nurse, hadn't worked full-time since she married my father, but she practiced her nursing at home and sometimes worked weekends at Braddock General Hospital.

As my mother's daughter, and as a child who grew up in hospitals, I knew all the clinical words for body parts and diseases. I never had colds, I had upper-respiratory infections. I did not have a belly button. I had an umbilicus. I knew the difference between a side-stitch and pleurisy, leg cramps and blood clots, code red and code blue. I could name viruses and cancers the way other kids could name constellations and state capitals. My mother read the *Physicians' Desk Reference* while her friends read cookbooks and romance novels. She diagnosed every fever, every sniff and cough.

But now, where my father was concerned, my mother sounded helpless.

"I don't know what he's trying to say," she said, her voice cracked and pleading, as if my father's survival depended upon my mother translating his Polish dream-speak, as if she had already failed.

My father, the son of immigrants, never taught me Polish or spoke it much in our home. He was embarrassed by his first language.

"I speak American," he'd say.

And now he'd returned to the language of his childhood, and my mother, who'd been married to him for over 40 years, couldn't understand the words.

Over the past year or so, on visits home, I noticed my father had lost weight, even though his appetite for covert sweets seemed stronger than ever. He had a pain in his back that seemed to be getting worse. He had a huge mole on his neck that he scratched until it bled. He'd been having recurring dreams, too, something he rarely did or at least didn't talk much about.

"The damnedest thing," he said. "This black dog shows up and carries a little yellow cat across this river. Night after night. Now what do you make of that, Miss College?"

My father, who helped pay my way through college, who was alternately proud and pissed off at all the education he felt I may have wasted, at all the education he'd given me that had never been offered to him, said, "What did they teach you about that in those schools of yours?"

I didn't talk to my father about Jung or Freud. I didn't talk about Hemingway, my beloved, who called depression Black Dog and who named his own dog Black Dog, and who died broken and sad.

I think I told my father I didn't know.

I think I said it was good he was dreaming.

As much as he didn't believe in a dream life or talk much about his dreams, my father loved to gamble—stocks, Vegas, the Pennsylvania Lottery. He'd bought a book, *The Success Dream Book* by someone named Prof. De Herbert. The book promised to match images from dreams with winning lottery numbers. In the introduction, Prof. De Herbert, who wrote his last name in all caps, declared his book the most complete dream book in the world.

"The author has worked laboriously and unceasingly in order to produce this first-class Dream Book," he wrote back in 1959. "He has traveled all over the world to gather correct data. There is nothing miraculously attached to this book: It is truly a dream book of the highest order and enables you to get all the main facts of your life at a glance."

Prof. De Herbert, who may have been the Donald Trump of prognosticators, called dreams—good or bad—warnings. The book was illustrated with questionable images of turbaned fortune tellers and mosques, crystal balls and genies. Along with dream interpretations, it included lucky birthday numbers, lucky holiday numbers, and a list called "Notions: Things You See, Hear or Happen and What to Do With Them." The list linked lottery numbers with events from waking life.

"When you are surprised by—367"

"When your left eye jumps—376"

"When your right eye jumps—659"

"When you see a riot—293"

"Sudden grief—144"

I don't know where Prof. De Herbert got his ideas or where my father found this book, but I know my father never won the Pennsylvania Lottery. He kept a record of winning lottery numbers, along with his losing tickets and *The Success Dream Book*, in a shoebox he stashed under our kitchen table. He'd pull the box out to show visitors how close he'd come, how many times he'd nearly hit.

"Almost," he'd say, again, again.

"Now what do you make of that?" my father wanted to know about his losing streaks, and now about his dream.

In *The Success Dream Book*, a black dog in a dream "denotes a dangerous adventure." Play number 371.

A cat is "a sign of approaching danger." Play 144.

Yellow: "Success in all undertakings." Play 336.

A river: "Strife and ill luck." Play 419.

Every number, even 419, was supposed to bring good luck. Prof. De Herbert wasn't much for irony.

My mother, a trained medical professional, was superstitious, too. She read horoscopes. She read "Dear Abby." I think she sometimes consulted *The Success Dream Book*, but she didn't admit that.

My mother believed she possessed psychic powers and was part bohemian. She was certain my father's dream was an omen.

"He didn't tell you Mitch Paitch was in that dream, did he?" my mother said.

Mitch Paitch was a name I hadn't heard in years. He was one of my father's few friends from the old neighborhood—someone who remembered when my father drank bourbon and sang Cole Porter songs and dressed up to take my mother dancing at The Belvedere Club or The White Elephant.

I remember Mitch Paitch and my father one night on our porch. I'm not sure how old I was, but I was in our backyard, trying as usual to fill a mayonnaise jar with lightning bugs. Citronella candles burned on the porch steps. They didn't do much to stop mosquitoes, but they were the only source of light other than the red tip of my father's and Mitch's cigarettes, which bobbed and glowed as the two men tried out some bars of a song I didn't know.

"Christ, Paitch," my father said. "What are you, deaf?"

"Look who's talking," Mitch said. "Married life killed your voice, all that bitching and moaning."

Mitch Paitch died decades ago. My father never talked about him much. My mother lost touch with his wife.

"It's strange for him to just show up in a dream," my mother said. "It's no good."

To dream of a friend, *The Success Dream Book* says, is "to wish for the peace of a well-trained person. Play 259." What Prof de Herbert meant by a well-trained person, or the peace that came with that, I don't know.

Maybe he meant someone who knew the realities, which is what Hemingway called life, the truth that everything and everyone we love is temporary, the peace that comes if we can live with the cruel beauty of that.

"Forget your personal tragedy," Hemingway wrote in a letter to his friend, F. Scott Fitzgerald, in 1934. "We are all bitched from the start, and you have to hurt like hell before you can write seriously. But when you get the damned hurt use it—don't cheat with it. Be as faithful to it as a scientist—but don't think anything is of any importance because it happens to you or anyone belonging to you."

Before we knew my father was very sick, his back pain had gotten so bad he couldn't sleep. He kept my mother up all night, too. My father hated doctors and I can imagine what went down between my mother and father before she convinced him to go.

The doctor ran some tests and decided my father needed surgery.

"The damnedest thing," my father said. "The doctor said he usually sees this in young men, never in men my age. A goddamn disc. I told you I'm going to live to a hundred. I'm going to be around. Hell, my back doesn't even know how old it is."

I came home the morning of my father's surgery. I was still in my flight attendant uniform, blue polyester suit, red silk scarf, wheeling my squeaky suitcase which left a black trail on Forbes Hospital's just-waxed floor. When I entered the waiting room, my mother saw me and began to cry.

When the doctors opened my father, they found cancer, not a disc problem. The cancer had spread from my father's lungs to his spine. The liver, the doctors said, was involved. The brain, too.

"He's still unconscious," my mother said. "He doesn't know yet."

My mother and I were there when my father woke up, groggy from the drugs, but still proud because he believed he was suffering a young man's disease.

"The damnedest thing," he said and smiled at me.

I can't remember how much time passed before my father was fully conscious, before I had to tell him what had gone wrong. My mother couldn't do it. I didn't want it left to the doctors, the sweet nurses.

"Dad," I said. "It wasn't a disc."

He didn't believe me. He didn't believe the doctors when they came in with their charts and diagnoses and treatment plans. He made a nurse write the words "metastasized adenocarcinoma, both lungs" on a piece of paper. He looked at the paper, with its ad for a new blood pressure drug, then folded it into a neat square.

"Put that in my wallet," he said, and I did.

Later, after my father died, my mother would find it there, tucked behind his driver's license. Later, when my mother died, I'd find it in her wallet, in the hidden space where she kept a $50 bill for emergencies and a medallion of The Virgin Mary she'd had blessed in Rome.

I'm leaping time again.

Forgive me.

Back in my father's hospital room, my mother wanted to know how long her husband, my father—one of so many other husbands, so many other fathers in the hospital at that moment, in so many other hospitals everywhere—would live. She pulled the doctors aside, one by one. They hedged. They consulted charts. Finally, she cornered one of the nurses.

"I know you know," my mother said. "I'm a nurse. Tell me. How long?"

"We can't be sure, we can never be sure," the nurse said.

"How long?" my mother, who already knew the answer, said.

"Usually a year," the nurse said, and looked down at her watch.

Time grounds us all, maybe.

Maybe the opposite.

My mother wore her watch with the face on the inside of her wrist, at her pulse point. Many nurses do this. The inside of a wrist, that tender place, the skin a membrane, rice paper, all those veins, the *vena amoris*, the vein that connects the hand to the heart.

Look at your wrist, those bridges of veins.

Feel the pulse.

How does time feel for you?

How does time connect to your own heart?

Tell me, please.

From that point on, I came home on my off days.

Sometimes I'd wake in hotel rooms and not know which city I was in. Sometimes, I'd wake in my pink childhood bedroom back in Trafford. Some days, if my father had a bad night, I'd lie awake on a small sofa next to the rented hospital bed we'd set up in my mother's old sewing room. Sometimes I'd let myself think about how many people had rented that bed before my father, or how many people had slept in the hotel beds I'd slept in all over the world. I still imagine the stories, all the love and loneliness embedded in these intimate everyday objects, all the small details of living and dying.

But there, in my mother's sewing room, I tried not to think too much. I listened to my father's breathing. A few years later, I'd listen to my mother's breathing. Many years later, I'd listen to my children's breathing. And my husband's breathing. Everyone I've loved. As if lying awake listening to them breathe—inhale, exhale—as if syncing my breath to theirs and placing my hand on their chests could keep them with me forever.

Back when my father was dying, my world shrank to small spaces—an airplane cabin, the low ceilings and tiny rooms in my parents' house, a taxicab, a single bed in my crash pad apartment in New York, a hotel bathtub.

If I was away for a week, I'd come home to find my father changed. He took chemo cocktails and radiation treatments. There were more and more pills for my mother to look up in *The Physicians' Desk Reference.* Each time, I wasn't sure what to expect when I'd ring my parents' doorbell and wait for someone to undo all the chain locks and bolts my father installed on our front door to keep everyone he loved safe.

It took a while.

A few weeks into chemo, my father started wearing an old knit cap he'd kept from his Navy days. He'd worn that cap as a crew member on *The Lexington*, a World War II aircraft carrier that had been in the Pacific. That cap and my father survived kamikazes and air strikes and storms at sea. It didn't matter that it was now Spring, that western Pennsylvania humidity had already set in.

When I pulled up one day in a taxi, my father was there, under the hood of his Chrysler, a sky-blue classic from the 1960s that felt bigger than my New York apartment. That car took my parents and me from Pittsburgh to Florida too many times to count. I would stretch out in the back and sleep my way across state lines while my parents bickered over routes and traffic and when and where to stop for gas.

My father loved that car. He waxed it with Turtle Wax once a week, even though, aside from Florida trips, he rarely drove it. Even near death, my father couldn't help tinkering.

"You take good care of a car, it will run forever," my father liked to say.

This day, my father's blue knit cap was pulled low over his eyebrows. He was wearing his old work clothes, a uniform stained with grease and graphite I thought retired with him after he left his job at Radform Tool, a tiny machine shop in a town called Wall.

My father, usually happy to see me, barely looked up.

"Your mother's inside," he said.

Every time I came home, both my parents looked smaller, more fragile, painfully mortal. It terrified me. I felt embarrassed by my fear, by the arrogance of my younger healthy body, and so I'd catch myself not looking at my parents straight on. I'd focus my eyes a bit above their heads, like I was fascinated by something on a wall–a clock, a calendar, a splotch of grease. I worried my parents would notice. I worried they could read my thoughts, all that darkness.

In the kitchen, my mother, bent like a comma over the sink, was peeling carrots and potatoes for a pork roast, one of the few things my father still wanted to eat. I kissed the top of her gray head. Then I focused on the kitchen cabinets. They needed cleaning. The stove did, too.

"What's with dad and the hat?" I asked.

"His hair," my mother said. "He's upset about his hair."

When he was young, my father had thick, dark, wavy hair. I'd seen pictures, but my father's hair had been mostly gone for years.

My father, his brothers, and most of the old Polish men I knew in Pittsburgh looked like John Paul II, the Polish Pope. They were almost completely bald, except for spidery strands of white hair they'd grow long, then wear in comb-overs.

My father, in one of his final gestures of vanity, carried a comb in his back pocket. He kept a can of hairspray in the bathroom. Aqua Net, I think.

That night and going forward, I never saw my father without his cap. He wore it through dinner when he picked at the tiny piece of roast on his plate. He wore it to watch the news. He wore it when he fell asleep on the couch. He wore it when my mother helped him to bed, and in the morning, there it was. He never said anything about it to me and I didn't say anything about it to him. Instead, I'd ask how he was feeling.

"What do you think, smartass?" he said. "Like shit. They're poisoning me."

On his nightstand, my father kept a prayer book, some cards, and news clippings neighbors cut out and sent, along with handwritten notes—"Try this" and "My sister did it and it works" and "Can't hurt"—touting the latest cancer miracle cures.

If there was an escape from death, my father would find it.

/ / \

Around the time my father laced all our doors with locks, he also did intricate mathematical equations to ensure the trees he planted in our yard would never—no matter how tall they grew—fall on our house or hurt anyone he loved.

Then he set up a nuclear fallout shelter in our basement.

This was the 1970s, the Cold War, and not so uncommon. The world is always terrifying, but sometimes more so.

My father, who knew war and death and had a commendation letter from Harry Truman hidden in his underwear drawer, built the shelter by hand with cement blocks he bought at Busy Beaver. He stacked the blocks in double layers and made walls within walls. He built a room within our laundry room. He outfitted the shelter with rows of wood shelves, then stocked them with huge cans of peanuts and creamed corn, boxes of beef jerky, and supplies of dog biscuits for our poodle, who would not be left behind in the event of war.

The shelves buckled under gallons of distilled water and Regent Pop. The basics my father couldn't buy at Foodland he mail-ordered from creepy survivalist magazines: a bottle of Minuteman Survival Tablets, camo tarps, and a huge bag of apricot pits.

The survival tablets—touted as "a compact lifesaving food ration fit for any emergency"—went into the bomb shelter, along with the tarps. The apricot pits went upstairs in our refrigerator's crisper drawer. My father ate a few every night.

According to the survivalist magazines, the pits had a bit of something awful in them—cyanide, I think—just enough to ward off cancer.

They didn't work, of course.

I tried some once. They were bitter and splintered between my teeth.

They tasted like dust.

"All are of the dust, and all turn to dust again." That's Ecclesiastes.

Of all parts of the Bible, I have always loved Ecclesiastes most. I thought it meant good news. The word feels like fireworks in your mouth. A celebration. Ecclesiastes! What a beautiful, lit-up word.

But in translation, Ecclesiastes is about the vanity of human life. All our joy. All our pain.

Temporary, my beloved Hemingway would say.

Maybe that's good news.

Maybe not.

\/\

"Do you know what that jackass said to me?" my father asked.

My father and I were sitting on the couch in my parents' living room, watching *60 Minutes.* It was an episode about Lance Armstrong, years before Sheryl Crow or those Livestrong bracelets or the doping scandals. The episode was all about the rock-star version of Lance Armstrong, Superhuman.

Lance Armstrong beat cancer, then went on to win the Tour de France three times, more. The episode was titled "Miracle Man."

The promo: "Lance Armstrong simply won't stop flirting with death."

My father had on his blue cap. He looked at the TV while he talked. I looked at the TV while he talked.

"That doctor," my father said. "He asked, 'How old are you? 75?' He said, 'Well then. You lived your life.' What the hell kind of thing is that to say to a person?"

On TV, Lance Armstrong was telling *60 Minutes'* Bob Simon about his "Cycle of Hope" campaign. Lance credited good doctors, good medicine, and good technology for his survival.

"20 years ago," Armstrong said. "I would've been dead."

"What kind of asshole says that kind of thing?" my father wanted to know about his own doctor.

I didn't say anything. I didn't know what to say.

On TV, Lance Armstrong, with his square rich-boy chin, expensive shirt, and loopy smile, was talking about hope.

"I knew there were people just diagnosed, or family members of people diagnosed, or survivors or people being treated," Armstrong said. "They were going to see me. They were going to say, 'That guy's one of us.' And they were going to get hope from that."

My father looked at me, straight on, in a way he hadn't in years. I made myself look at him straight on, too.

"I'm dying you know," he said.

"Yes," I said. "I know."

"There's no way out of it," my father said.

"Yes," I said. "I know."

"Okay then," he said, and we both turned back to the TV.

Hemingway said, "Every man's life ends the same way. It is only the details of how he lived and how he died that distinguish one man from another."

Years later, after my father died, Lance Armstrong was called the dirtiest cheater in the history of sports. He took enough performance-enhancing drugs to make a hippo fly. Those drugs made his super-human victories and survival seem attainable, beyond mortal.

60 Minutes, feeling guilty, would air four other segments debunking Armstrong and exposing his grand doping scheme and subsequent cover-up. Each time, Armstrong would call and threaten reporters, right up until Armstrong confessed to Oprah Winfrey, the world's priest and eater of sins. Armstrong told Oprah he used blood doping, transfusions, testosterone, human growth-hormone cocktails and more to elevate his strength and endurance for each Tour win from 1999 to 2005. He likened the drugs to "keeping air in his tires." He said he even looked up the word "cheat" in the dictionary and decided it didn't apply to him, given that it meant "to gain an advantage on a rival or foe."

"I didn't view (doping) that way," he told Oprah. "I viewed it as leveling the playing field."

"We absolutely helped create the myth," CBS News Chairman Jeff Fager said about *60 Minutes'* role in creating the hero version of Lance Armstrong. "We put Lance Armstrong on our broadcast in front of millions and millions of people. We called him Miracle Man. We wanted to believe it. Who didn't?"

"Don't worry about me, sweetheart," my father said. "I'll be around."

That was the last thing my father said to me before he died.

I believed it.

He was my father, my miracle.

I will forever be his child.

It was hard to find a place to be alone in my parents' house, so that night, after my father told me he knew he was dying, after he fell asleep on the couch, his head tilted back, snoring, I shut off the TV. I went down to the basement, where years ago my father had built a bathroom out of the cement blocks left over from his bomb shelter. He'd put a shower stall in there so he could take showers after work without tracking graphite through the house.

The work my father did in this life was filthy—his clothes filthy, his skin blackened, his lungs diseased. *Good jobs*, people who remember the mills and machine shops of Pittsburgh-past, say, meaning the jobs paid enough for people to live a while, a living wage.

I took a shower.

Then I sat on the floor of the makeshift shower stall.

Since my parents wouldn't be able to hear me, I let myself weep.

In the weeks before he died, my father asked my mother to sell his Chrysler. She did, for five hundred dollars to my uncle, my father's brother, who was sweet and rich and, according to family legend, one of the few Polish made-men in the Pittsburgh mob.

"No sense leaving it to rot," my father said about his car.

People started to come by. Cousins I hadn't seen in years, neighbors, my father's stockbroker, my father's bookie.

Growing up, I thought everyone had a bookie. I'd answer the phone when my father's bookie would call and say the words my father taught me and place a bet on a number that, in keeping with my father's luck, would never hit. My birthday in a box for a nickel. My mother's birthday in a box for fifty cents. Some number from *The Success Dream Book.*

When I was very young, my father's bookie would send me cards on my birthday. The cards would have trees on the front, with slots he'd fill with quarters or fifty-cent pieces on all the branches. He'd sign the card, "Your Fairy Godfather," but I always knew who it was, even though I never knew the bookie's name, such is the life of a bookie.

When he showed up at my father's death bed, the bookie looked different than I imagined. He was tiny, stooped, ancient, in a sky-blue polyester dress shirt, a pack of Pall Mall cigarettes in his chest pocket, pleated pants pulled up to his ribs and cinched with a belt.

My father's bookie looked like he shopped at JCPenney. He looked like an old man who'd sell ice cream from a street cart.

"He's a good man," the bookie said about my father, and shook my hand like we were making one last deal.

The bookie's hands were smooth, small, not like my father's hands, rough from years of work. The bookie's hands felt like he never hurt anyone, like he could never hurt anyone. Maybe he didn't. Maybe it was all just numbers and dreams. Maybe it was hand cream, something expensive rated five stars by bookies everywhere, who knows.

"I'll say the rosary for your dad," the bookie said. "I'll say a Novena for you, too, sweetheart."

I thanked him, even though I stopped believing years ago.

I thanked him because I wanted so much to believe.

My uncle—the made-man who bought my father's car—came every day.

My father wanted to talk mostly about Frank Sinatra, who, along with the movie critic Gene Siskel and King Hussein of Jordan, was also dying—cancer, cancer.

"That bastard," my father said about Sinatra. "He's afraid to go to sleep. I saw it on the news. He's afraid he won't wake up."

My father, who could sing like Sinatra, who loved Sinatra despite his mob ties, who loved his brother, my uncle, despite his mob ties, who loved his bookie despite mob ties, was afraid, too, though he wouldn't admit it.

"I'm a man," my father often said. "I'm a man and I know it."

People these days talk a lot about the patriarchy. But what my father meant was that to be a man meant being stoic. It meant being silent about things. "Grace under pressure," my beloved Hemingway, veteran of war and plane crashes and heartbreak, called it. To be a man, in my father's eyes, meant taking care of the people he loved. It meant not scaring people, even when you were dying, even when you were scared.

Cancer didn't kill Frank Sinatra, though he suffered from it. He had a massive heart attack instead.

Frank Sinatra's last words: "I'm losing."

For my father, people were always a problem, at the end even more so.

My father didn't trust the sweet hospice nurse, who was also a nun, who wore Winnie-the-Pooh socks and a large crucifix around her neck. He didn't want the hospital bed she'd ordered and all the ghosts that came with it. He didn't want the pills. He didn't trust my mother, who he feared would outlive him. My father wanted to die alongside my mother. He couldn't bear the idea of her going on without him.

"You're trying to kill me," he told her. "You want me dead."

When my mother would leave my father's sick room weeping, I tried to talk my father down, but he wouldn't have it.

"You don't know a damn thing," he'd say. "Little Miss College. What did they teach you about this, jackass? What's in those books of yours?"

Nothing.

Once, when a delivery man showed up with tanks of oxygen, my father was lying on the couch. I could see him sizing this young man up. The delivery man was probably in college. This job probably paid for his books.

"Let me ask you something," my father said.

The man, a boy really, wore paper boot covers on his shoes. His hair fell over one eye in a heartbreaking boy-band swoop. He carried a clipboard. He carried a Sharpie.

So many orders to deliver. So many people suffering.

My father glared at him.

"So," my father said, "how long do people live once you bring this stuff?"

The boy smiled, awkward, nervous. He held out the clipboard for someone, anyone to sign.

My father said, "Are you the angel of death?"

My father said, "How does that feel, doing a job like this?"

I signed the boy's clipboard.

"Thank you," I said. "Sorry."

I tipped him some.

How much tip is standard for the angel of death? Twenty percent, at least.

Then came the drug deliveries. The drugs kept getting stronger—Ativan, morphine.

"We want to keep him comfortable," the hospice nurse said. "We want him to be peaceful."

Peace, peaceful. There is no such thing as a good death. I've said that. So did Simone de Beauvoir, whose grave I visited in Paris. I love Simone de Beauvoir. She called death an aberration. Anyone who knows death knows she was right. No one can argue with the French about cheese or wine or mortality.

My father's death was anything but peaceful.

Before he died, my father went in and out of consciousness. My uncle, the made-man who could speak Polish, who spoke that native tongue with my father when they were children, was there for some of this.

He was there when my father tried to open a door he saw dangling above his rented hospital bed. He was there when my father cried out for their mother. He was there when my father went on speaking in Polish. He was there when my father began waving his hands near his mouth, tiny floating gestures, back and forth over his lips.

I hoped my uncle would translate for me, but he wouldn't.

"It's nonsense," my uncle said. "He doesn't know what he's saying."

My uncle is dead now too. Cancer. In his casket, he looked so much like my father. Whatever their relationship was like as children, whatever love they shared together, whatever fury, is lost to me. But back then, as my father was dying, my uncle's eyes filled with tears as he told me something I'd never known about my father.

"What happened to his harmonica?" my uncle asked.

The story goes, one Christmas, when my father was a teenager, my grandfather, in a moment of tenderness, bought my father, who loved music, a harmonica and a songbook. My uncle said for years my father never went anywhere without it.

"He'd sit on a stoop and play until I wanted to pull my ears off," my uncle said. "He'd play 'Red River Valley,' 'Oh Susanna.' You name it, he'd play it. All day. All night. He drove us all crazy."

I'd never seen this harmonica. I never heard my father mention it. But my mother remembered it, too.

"He used to sit on the porch and play and play," she said. "He'd sit there for hours in the dark, not talking to anybody. Just him and that damn harmonica. Gave me a goddamn headache. Useless."

My mother didn't know what happened to the harmonica. She couldn't remember when my father stopped playing.

After my father died, I expected to find it tucked in the pocket of an old jacket or hidden in a drawer somewhere, like his letter from Harry Truman, but it never showed.

I know when I try to tell you about my father, his harmonica, this is just a memory playing it as it lays. I know our brains create worlds we want to believe in. I want my father to have had beauty in his life, some private moments of joy, and so I imagine him, his breath gliding over notes, lifting music into the night sky.

When I remember that night my father spent with Mitch Paitch on our porch, I add in a harmonica that wasn't there to create more joy and happiness and beauty, especially that.

Maybe Lance Armstrong wasn't lying when he said he looked up the word "cheat" and believed it didn't apply to him.

"I didn't have anything else to lose," Lance Armstrong told *60 Minutes*. "That was the beautiful thing."

Lance Armstrong, by all accounts a lousy human, is still alive. He invested in Uber and made millions. He owns a café in Austin, Texas called Juan Pelota—One Ball, a joke in Spanish about his testicular cancer. On Lance Armstrong's Facebook page, for his bio, there's just one word. "Survivor."

Fuck you, Lance Armstrong.

Mitch Paitch, my father had figured out, was the dog in his dream.

"I was the cat," he said. "Mitch carried me. We were singing. I don't know what song. What do you make of that?"

In my memory, I'm there with my father and Mitch Paitch. I'm in my parents' yard. I'm at my gruesome business, ripping the lights from the poor bugs I've caught in my lightning jar. I crush their bodies, smash their abdomens into a yellow paste I rub on my arms and cheeks.

I don't think this is cruel. I think I'm Goldie Hawn in *Laugh-In*, a hippie with glowing flowers on her skin. I think I am a spirit, a ghost girl who wants to be beautiful.

I want my father to see me, the way I can still see him, a beacon, his cigarette, a small heart keeping a beat in the dark.

In my dreams, I run to my father. I cry, *Can you see me?* I want my father to sing. I want him to tell me what an asshole I am and always will be. I want to hear his harmonica. I want him to be happy.

"What do you want now, Miss College?"

I want to cover us all in light.

God Damn It, Be Kind

My daughter Phelan liked to dress up as a character she created herself, a professional wrestler named Violent Violet Jones.

"It's all about story," she said when she talked about why she loved professional wrestling while most of the other girls at her school loved boy bands and American Girl Dolls and overpriced sequin-y clothes from a store called Justice.

"It's about good guys and bad guys," Phelan said. "It's scripted, not fake."

I love that my then-14-year-old daughter considered this, the complexity of the world up against the ease most people believe in. When people asked how my sweet, smart daughter got into wrestling, I would shrug and smile. No one else in our family was into it, though I remember my father loving Andre the Giant and Pittsburgh legend Bruno Sammartino when I was growing up.

My father died years before Phelan was born. He loved Andre because Andre was an outsider and sad but kind. He loved Bruno because Bruno was Pittsburgh and a good son who loved his mother. Both represented hope. My father didn't see much goodness in the world.

"I'll live to see the bastards burn," he said, meaning most people.

Hope, even the bastard-burning kind, helped my father live, the way it helps all of us, I think.

My daughter was and still is the embodiment of hope. She is almost always joyful. One day when she was 11, she walked into her bedroom, shut the door, came out hours later, and asked her father, "Do you know who Larry Zbyszko is?" and he said, "The wrestler?" and Phelan, all blonde curls, her voice like sparkling juice, proceeded to spout statistics.

We love when our kids discover worlds we never imagined.

"The Heart wants what it wants," Emily Dickinson wrote.

But writers are my business, not my daughter's.

My daughter's young heart loved men who leapt from the top rope and smashed each other.

As for Violent Violet Jones, she was half-Harlequin, half pin-up girl.

Phelan's best friend Cilia, a future fashion designer and artist, made the costume out of clothes they found together at Goodwill. What had been someone's old prom dress transformed into satin shorts and a halter-top. What had been someone's scarf was now a championship belt. A polyester skirt the color of a juice stain—something a 1980s businesswoman might have worn with Leggs suntan pantyhose and a blazer with oven mitts for shoulder pads—became boot covers and fingerless gloves.

"Ba-Boom!" my daughter said when she strutted through our tiny house like it was a runway. She did an impressive sidekick and struck a pose. "Do you like it?" she asked.

Cilia is a brilliant seamstress, but the outfit was pretty revealing, in a bathing suit kind of way. Lots of stomach. Young boobs coming out. A little butt.

"You are not letting her go out like that," my son Locklin said. He was 17 then, and knew some things but not others. He hated professional wrestling, mostly because his sister loved it. He worried. Years later, he worries still about what people think and how every thought reflects back on him. He worries constantly. He looks at his phone. He worries more.

Locklin said, "You are not letting her go out like that."

"Of course I am," I said, and scowled at him. "She can wear what she wants."

"I look pretty okay," Phelan said, tossing her long blonde curls over one shoulder then the other while her brother sighed and stared at the ceiling and hoped we'd notice and put a stop to all this.

"You look awesome. So badass," I said, and hugged Violent Violet Jones hard.

"Clueless," Locklin said to the ceiling, to the dust bunnies hanging there, and I pretended not to hear.

My son still frustrates me with his fears. I pretend that's not so because I am his mother and filled with fears of my own.

But back then, I gave in. I went to Target and bought Phelan two full body suits—one black, one beige—to go underneath her wrestling costume.

As women, we try to love our bodies, even so. But we forget the danger of other people, men, loving our bodies too much.

"So you're not cold," I said, and passed her a sweater and a pair of my combat boots.

Phelan turned 14 that July, but she looked older. She was beautiful but didn't know how beautiful. She is even more beautiful now, nearing the end of her teens, but she still doesn't know how beautiful.

I want her to be free to become her own good badassed self, but I am not clueless.

One of Violent Violet Jones' signature moves was The Baby Kick, something my daughter started doing when she was just out of diapers and still helpless. She learned it while roughhousing with my husband. She used to lie on her back and kick hard. It was hilarious. She used her heels to do damage.

At 14, she still wanted to baby kick.

I pretended nothing about her was sexual while knowing it was and will be sexual, sexy, creepy, not creepy, pretty.

Pretty is the right word, I think.

"Be safe. Stay with your friends," I said to my daughter as she headed out for what would likely be her last round of trick-or-treating, her childhood fading into ether.

"Don't go to strangers' houses. Don't get into any cars. Watch for creeps."

"I know, I know," she said, and kissed me hard, four times, exactly four times, something she did and will go on doing for luck.

"It always has to be four," she said, though she can't say how she decided that.

Things that come in fours:

Suits in a deck of cards.

Teenage Mutant Ninja Turtles.

The Four Horsemen of the Apocalypse.

When I was young, I told my parents I loved them all the time. I did it so often things got weird.

"Pass the salt, please, I love you."

"I can't find this sock, please, I love you."

One time my father asked me why. I told him I wanted "I love you" to be the last thing he'd hear before he died.

He quit speaking to me.

My father hated the idea of death, mortality. He wanted to believe he would never die. The idea of death scared him, but I didn't know that then.

I felt sad and confused. Young, blameless, I believed in death. I believed everyone I loved would drop over at any minute and I, the adopted kid, would be twice orphaned.

Ba-boom. Just like that.

"As it was in the beginning, so it will be in the end," Father Ackerman, the hairy-eared priest at St. Regis often said.

Father Ackerman was famous for shouting kids down in confessionals and prescribing three thousand Hail Marys and Our Fathers to clean out sins. He told me I'd go to Hell multiple times.

But I believed if I did the right things, if I was good enough, if I knew the proper magic, the correct words in the correct order, I could save people.

I could even save myself.

Even now, when my daughter kisses me, I think about my friend Maggie. As a child, Maggie would make herself say "peace and love" eleven times before she would fall asleep at night. Like me, Maggie was sure everyone she loved would die if she didn't do things just right.

"I had OCD before OCD was a thing," she says now and laughs.

Lately, my daughter holds my face in her soft hands when she kisses me.

"Hold still," she says.

Maggie's mother died when Maggie was 17.

Both my parents are dead now.

My father's last words to me were, "Don't worry, honey, I'll be around."

My mother's last words were, "Is that all?"

She had asked what time it was, and I told her and she was disappointed it wasn't later, as if her death was on a schedule, as if it were a train running behind.

I don't remember my last words to my father, but with my mother, it was just that, the time.

11 a.m., give or take.

According to numerology, the number 11 is the angel number, a communication from God. When you see the number 11 on your alarm clock, prepare your heart, mind, and body for tremendous acts of grace.

"Magical thinking," psychologists call it.

If you see "11:11" on your clock, tell the people you love that you love them.

If you see "11:11" on your clock, make a wish.

It's a talisman, maybe. A touchstone.

Another way for people to go on.

Four days before Halloween, as my daughter planned her first transformation into Violent Violet Jones, a man murdered 11 people at The Tree of Life synagogue in Squirrel Hill.

"Unthinkable," journalists called it, but that's not right.

Nearly a year earlier, another gunman killed 26 worshipers at a church in Sutherland Springs, Texas. Nearly a year before that, a white supremacist killed nine parishioners in a church in Charleston, South Carolina. And on. And on.

What's unthinkable: that beauty can exist alongside horror, sometimes in the same place and time.

Squirrel Hill is 20 minutes from my house. On most Saturdays, Phelan and I were there, a few blocks from the synagogue. She took music lessons at a place called Sunburst.

Sunburst on Saturday mornings was filled with children laughing, exhausted parents sighing over coffee they snagged from a shop downstairs, the sound of music drifting from the practice rooms.

I liked sitting in the lobby for the 30 minutes my daughter spent singing and laughing with her teacher, a pretty rosebud woman named Roseanna who played in a duo with her husband when she wasn't teaching kids. Roseanna and her husband played a lot of weddings and bar mitzvahs. Their music was sweet and uplifting and helped people.

"To me every hour of the light and dark is a miracle," Walt Whitman, believing in people and miracles despite people, said.

My daughter adored Roseanna. Roseanna encouraged Phelan to write songs, then Roseanna sang backup and played piano to my daughter's songs at recitals.

It was so beautiful I could have screamed.

The receptionist at Sunburst was a musician, too. I used to see her perform around Pittsburgh back in the '90s. She controlled the background music in the lobby, and I loved everything she picked—The Replacements, The Clash, The Verve, Counting Crows' *August and Everything After*.

I moved away from Pittsburgh in the '90s. I went to New York, which is what people from Pittsburgh often do when we want to become writers and artists. We believe in the magic of New York, its glitter and shine, its promise of transformation. Plus, it's drivable, just 7 hours away.

"I went to New York City to be born again," Kurt Vonnegut said.

I went to New York City to be born again. And then there was 9/11, the exodus after that.

I moved back to Pittsburgh just before 9/11. I'd been a flight attendant. What 9/11 means to me is something I haven't found words for yet. I didn't lose anyone close to me, which means no one close to me died in one of those planes or in the towers. People close to me were there, though. People close to me were changed forever, the way the city I loved was changed forever, but I was already an outsider, and I don't have a right to that story, however painful and personal it feels.

Back then, my father was dying, my mother needed help. I moved home. I planned to go back to New York, my beloved, but I didn't, which is what Pittsburghers do, I think, regardless. It's what I did. Pittsburghers. We come home. We come home and stay.

Beloved.

Beloved.

"Like homing pigeons," a man in a New York bar once told me about Pittsburghers. "You leave. You go back. You're lucky. There aren't many places like that."

He was from South Carolina, I think.

A few of my Pittsburgh friends are displaced New Yorkers who came to Pittsburgh for an easier, kinder, gentler, safer life.

Pittsburgh, the birthplace of bingo and Ferris wheels.

Pittsburgh, the neighborhood of the Rooneys and the Steelers and Mister Rogers.

"There are three ways to ultimate success," Mister Rogers used to say. "The first way is to be kind. The second way is to be kind. The third way is to be kind."

I believe that. I also know the world can be a terrible place.

After Tree of Life, Pittsburgh became known as a place where an armed anti-Semite slaughtered 11 people who had come together in love and peace.

Around the time the synagogue shooting happened, Tom Hanks was in Pittsburgh filming a movie about Mister Rogers. There were pictures in the news: Tom Hanks looking earnest in Mister Rogers' sweater and Keds; Tom Hanks explaining death to puppets; X the Owl using reason to calm Henrietta Pussycat and coming up short.

Later in the news, reporters would latch onto the fact that Squirrel Hill was Mister Rogers' real neighborhood. He lived just a few blocks away and walked the sidewalks and got coffee and shopped at Little's Shoes.

The news reported this like it meant the death of something.

Kindness and hope, maybe.

On September 13, 2001, Graydon Carter, the editor of *Vanity Fair*, declared irony dead.

On September 14, 2001, *Onion* editor Stephen Thomson said, "None of us are feeling funny. The age of irony is dead."

Writers and theorists and politicians battled for ownership of the idea. Andrew Coyne in Canada's *National Post* coined it on September 12, a full day before Graydon Carter.

"The Age of Irony died yesterday," Coyne wrote.

The New York Time's Roger Rosenblatt wrote on September 24: "One good thing could come from this horror: it could spell the end of the age of irony."

It went on and on, as if irony's death could save us all.

"I can't go on," Irish playwright Samuel Beckett said years before all that. "I go on."

A week after 9/11, I flew back to New York to be with my friend Carol. Carol and I met when we were hired at Delta Air Lines. She is one of my most beloveds. We flew together whenever we could and made it our mission to be kind to people.

Carol was in the air when planes flew into the towers, into the Pentagon. Her husband, Rob, was a New York cop. He worked the pile, which is what people called the site where the towers used to stand.

Carol, my sweetest friend, is from Pittsburgh, like me. Carol is a cool customer. She said she was fine. Fine. I didn't believe her and so I flew in, and we spent days walking circles around her Long Island neighborhood. Rob would come home with baggies filled with things he'd found on the pile. A postcard, some pictures, a letter, a toothbrush. He was trying to find anyone connected to the things he found. He couldn't believe people were gone, while these things, these ordinary things, survived.

Time capsules.

Rob drank a lot when I was there, a few six packs a night.

Carol and I drank a lot when I was there because what else was there to do? Let's toast to the death of irony? Dear God, nothing was about that. There are ideas. And then there are people. Lives.

Everywhere in New York, there were flyers and posters: "Have you seen?" "Beloved father and husband." "Our mother." "Please contact."

"Please."

The man who killed those people in the Tree of Life synagogue was driven by hate, of course. The news reports said he told the police who captured him that he wanted to kill all the Jews.

The doctors in Pittsburgh who worked hardest to save his life were Jewish.

"Ain't that a kick in the ass," an anonymous hospital source said.

"I wish I could believe in things I used to believe in," I said to my husband the other day.

"I'm relieved I don't believe in things I used to believe in." I said that, too.

We'd been talking about time, about growing old, about the world, what that does to a person.

We've been together almost 20 years. We're both writers. Pittsburgh is our beloved home country.

We believe in the power of words.

We know words can't save anyone.

Recently, the family of Cecil and David Rosenthal, two brothers in their 50s who were killed in the Tree of Life shooting, placed a full-page advertisement in *The Pittsburgh Post-Gazette.* The ad urged people to perform random acts of kindness for strangers.

The ad said the brothers, who were both special needs and by all accounts the gentlest of hearts, left a legacy of love, kindness, and acceptance. The ad featured a drawing of the brothers, and "Random Acts of Kindness" coupons readers could cut out and share with strangers.

"Be committed to making your community a better place, and make a stranger's day," the coupons say. "Be creative. Be passionate. Be stronger than hate."

The family set up a Facebook page where people could share stories of kindness. The page is called "Love Like the Boys." The first picture there is of a little girl named Paisley. She looks about 11, maybe. Paisley has a huge white bow in her hair. She's holding a Random Acts of Kindness coupon. She wears a shirt that says, "I Am Woman Hear Me Roar."

Kurt Vonnegut wrote this, too: "Hello babies. Welcome to Earth. It's hot in the summer and cold in the winter. It's round and wet and crowded. On the outside, babies, you've got a hundred years here. There's only one rule that I know of babies. God damn it, you've got to be kind."

It was "Dress Up as A Superhero" day at my daughter's school, something to do with the D.A.R.E. program which was supposed to keep kids off drugs and inspire them to be their own good selves.

Phelan wanted to wear her Violent Violet Jones costume. "Even though no one will get it," she said.

We worried over dress codes, too much skin, her brother's eye-rolling, but we made it work.

I went out to warm up the car, the way I did every winter morning. I drove my daughter to school because she didn't like the bus so early in the day— too loud, too much, she liked to stay quiet in the morning. She liked time to think her thoughts.

"All those crazy kids," she said and waved a hand as if she were not one of them.

At the entrance to her school, there were new signs that said, "Gun-free school zone" and "School grounds under surveillance."

These were the first things we saw every day. I wanted to stop and take a picture of the signs, but I never did. I don't know why I wanted to document them. Proof, maybe. Of this world and its terrors. But anyone who reads the news knows. Anyone who is a parent knows. We go on despite the knowing. Mostly that.

That day, I pulled up to the front doors, where Phelan had to stand in front of a camera and buzz in and state her name and grade before the door buzzed open with a sound that will always remind me of a prison. Her school, like most schools now, had active-shooter drills and evacuations and there was a grim police officer stationed most days inside the entrance, for which I'm both sad and grateful.

I always waved to him. Sometimes he waved back.

My daughter checked her make-up in the visor mirror. She woke up early to do her eyes to match her costume, glittering in every shade of purple. Her lips were a shade called Jinx.

She snapped the visor up and turned to me.

"How do I look?" she asked and sucked in her cheeks and puckered up. "Do I look okay?"

I look for hope and kindness everywhere I can find it.

Most often I find it in my daughter's face, then, now, her love for the world and the strange and wonderful things in it: wrestling, a song, the color purple, all royalty and bruises, the magic of being alive.

"The world breaks everyone," Hemingway said. "And afterward many are strong at the broken places."

I love Hemingway. He knew things I try to know. *The realities*, a critic once said.

"You look so beautiful," I said, and leaned into my daughter, who kissed me four times hard.

Things that come in fours: nucleotides, the seasons, the sign of the cross.

I want us to go on like this forever and ever.

I want even now to tell my daughter the world is as beautiful as she believes, but terrifying and hard, too.

But I didn't say any of this that day. That day, my daughter left four kiss marks the color of amethyst, the color of mountain laurel and lilac, on my cheeks and forehead.

With Great Power Comes Great Responsibility

When he was young, my son Locklin loved Spiderman because Spiderman told jokes and saved people.

Being a kid feels helpless. Peter Parker was a kid, too. People thought he was powerless and weak, but he wasn't.

And so, when Locklin was in kindergarten, he took a Sharpie to a red turtleneck and scrawled the letters H.S. on the chest. H.S. for Human Spider.

"Not Spiderman?" I said, and my son looked at me like I'd accused him of plagiarism.

H.S., Locklin informed me, was his own superhero, completely unique, not derivative.

Never mind that the inkblot squiggled beneath the Sharpie'd letters looked like it was sprouting spider legs. Never mind that my son made a twip-twip noise that sounded a lot like web shooters whenever he was wearing the shirt.

"I'll save you," my son said as he swooped in and out of rooms, a flash of red, a blonde shock of hair, a whirlwind of salvation whooshing on invisible threads through our house.

My firstborn only son.

The miracle of that.

Once, when I was volunteering at Trafford Elementary's Fun Day, an annual thing where the school brings in huge inflatable bouncy houses and magicians and clowns to celebrate the end of the school year, Locklin's teacher, Mr. O, pulled me aside.

It was almost 90 degrees and my job had been to hand out bottles of water and try to help the less athletic kids make it up and over an inflatable climbing wall without weeping. I wasn't supposed to give the kids a boost, rules about touching and all, so my job was to say, "You got this! You can do it!" over and over.

Most of the kids couldn't do it.

I'd started to wonder if the climbing wall was coated with Vaseline the way they'd just slide right off. Some of the kids would run and lunge, tongues sticking out the sides of their mouths, fingers and toes clawing at hot rubber. They'd make it maybe halfway, then slip and tumble backwards onto the bouncy house floor, where they'd lie like dead beetles until I scuttled them away.

I blamed video games. I still do.

"It's Locklin," Mr. O said. "He won't take it off."

"Take what off?" I said as one of the downed kids started to thrash and wail.

Mr. O said, "The turtleneck. I'm afraid he's going to overheat."

Locklin, it turned out, had snuck out of the house with his H.S. turtleneck in his backpack. He put it on in the school bathroom. He was on duty as H.S. and would not be daunted by weather or teachers. The world, these kids, needed him.

The downed kids on the bouncy house floor, for instance.

Mr. O took over climbing-wall duty while I went to find my son. When I found him, he was dripping sweat, perched like an adorable gargoyle on top of the school's monkey bars, keeping watch.

"Those kids," he said, pointing at the bouncy house where the bodies were piling up. "They can't climb like me."

"Sweetheart," I said. "Come down. You don't need to wear the shirt to be a hero."

"But how will they know I'm a good guy?" he said.

"They'll know you're a good guy because you're good," I said, coaxing him to the ground, where I shuffled him off to the bathroom to change.

Spiderman was a deep thinker. With great power comes great responsibility and all that.

"All these years, I've done my best," he tells Aunt May. "But no matter how hard I try, people die."

"Don't ever die," my son said to me when he was very young, still says.

"I love you," I said to my parents, over and over. "I want that to be the last thing you hear before you die."

"I'll save you," my son said, still says.

He has.

He does.

"I love you," my son yells whenever he's leaving the house. He'll yell it again and again until I and his father yell it back, a pact, a promise, a covenant even.

My son is 19 years old when I'm diagnosed.

When he hears I have cancer, he melts.

Part 3

Say You Want to Live and Be Beautiful

A Memoir of a Diagnosis

"The standard cure for one who is sunk is to consider those in actual destitution or physical suffering. But at three o'clock in the morning, a forgotten package has the same tragic importance as a death sentence, and the cure doesn't work—and in a real dark night of the soul it is always three o'clock in the morning."

—F. Scott Fitzgerald, "The Crack-Up"

"Forget your personal tragedy. We are all bitched from the start and you have to hurt like hell before you can write seriously. But when you get the damned hurt use it—don't cheat with it."

—Ernest Hemingway, Letter to F. Scott Fitzgerald,
Sent from Key West, 28 May 1934

"All life is a process of breaking down."

—F. Scott Fitzgerald, "The Crack-Up"

"Jesus it's marvelous to tell other people how to write, live, die etc."

—Ernest Hemingway Letter to F. Scott Fitzgerald,
Sent from Key West, 28 May 1934

"I avoided writers very carefully. They can perpetuate trouble as no one else can."

—F. Scott Fitzgerald, "The Crack-Up"

PROLOGUE

This is about cancer.

Mine.

I don't mean to brag.

Except for the Cancer, I'm Fine

Chapter 1

A creek in my hometown—Trafford, Pennsylvania—used to run orange with sulfur and mine drainage, and the air near the creek smelled like rotten eggs, some days more than others.

The fish that came from the creek were catfish, deformed, pox-ridden, with huge, panicked eyes. My friends and I would find them washed-up, dead. We'd poke them with sticks until they'd spurt.

This was our childhood. We thought it magic. We found abandoned refrigerators near the creek and tried to commandeer them into boats that would take us away—where, we had no idea. The refrigerators sank. Everything we thought might float sank into the muck and orange of the poisoned water of our home.

Older people fished in the creek anyway. I don't know if they ate the fish. They probably did, because people were out of work and living on government butter and cheese in the 1900s, the '70s and '80s and '90s specifically.

My friends and I waded and swam in that creek.

One of my oldest friends, Donnie, who suffers from MS now, has the best collection of sulfur creek glass ever. Sulfur creek glass is beautiful, like amber, but it's mostly broken brown beer bottles and broken green beer bottles worn smooth by toxic water. Our people's version of sea glass.

Worthless, people say, about beautiful things that can't be converted to cash.

There is no such thing as a natural sulfur creek, though I didn't know that growing up.

Our town's creek has a real name: Turtle Creek. Sometimes my friends and I found box turtles. Sometimes the box turtles were deformed like the fish. There was a rumor that someone knew someone who knew someone who found a turtle with two heads.

We knew it was important to never move a box turtle from where we found it. Box turtles travel a mile in their lifetimes. If they're moved from their birthplace, they wander forever, heartbroken, trying to get back to that one mile that first gained access to their hearts.

"The purpose of all art," Camus said, "is to gain access to what first gained access to our hearts."

I love Camus. I repeat him like a mantra.

I keep repeating things I love because those things tether me to this life.

Do not ever move a box turtle from where you've found it.

Thank you, amen.

"You Pittsburgh people," that man in a bar in New York told me way back, remember? "You're homing pigeons. You go away. You go back. You die in the place you were born. End of story."

I wanted to tell him, "Box turtles," but I was drinking and didn't feel like explaining much.*

*Earlier in this book, I made this man more polite than he was about Pittsburgh. This version feels right, but again: drinking. Forgive me.

My friends and I always came out of the water, our refrigerator boats sunk, our skin stained orange.

We thought sulfur creeks were something natural—fresh water, salt water, sulfur water. Such is the life of kids growing up in a dying mill town.

We didn't think much about the future because planning was for the rich.

That guy in the New York bar? He was drinking $12 martinis. He wore a scarf, a silk/wool blend probably, not itchy like it should be.

And yet I am back in the place where I started, as he predicted.

"So what," said Andy Warhola, who rose from Pittsburgh soil but wanted the world to believe he was from New York.

"Whatever," Andy Warhol said at his Factory, after he dropped the "a" from his name.

My mother couldn't have children of her own. That's what people called it then: children of her own.

My aunt couldn't have children of her own. Many people I knew couldn't have children of their own, and many of my friends growing up were adopted, like me.

Everyone from our town seemed to end up with health problems—lupus, thyroid trouble, MS like Donnie. I would guess most people born here die from cancer, with drunk-driving accidents a not-close second.

Who would ever care about a turtle wandering lost from the rusted-out waters of Turtle Creek in Trafford, Pennsylvania?

I loved being in the orange water.

All of us did.

Kids used to glue glitter and sequins on the backs of turtles they found. They'd weigh the turtles down with bedazzling and Gorilla Glue, then set the turtles free, left to wander, glittering, lonely, longing for somewhere familiar, somewhere like home, somewhere safe to die.

When you're waiting for a call about cancer, your mind wanders.

I hope you don't know this. I'm sorry if you do.

Strangers in bars. Childhood. These are the kinds of things you think about. Or I think about. I say *you* because I want not to be alone in this. I have a lot invested in believing I'm not alone in this because I feel alone in this.

Fucking cancer.

Growing up in Trafford, a Westinghouse town, a town of labor and industry, the word terrified everyone I knew so much they'd whisper it, if they said it at all.

Those poor turtles.

I can barely swim.

Forgive me my indulgence.

Cancer is so common, scientific terms for it show up in crossword puzzles. Cancer is often the answer to questions on *Jeopardy.*

Cancer, the big C, is so common it's hardly worth mentioning, maybe.

I grew up in the Catholic Church, St. Regis, located in downtown Trafford. St. Regis is a church in the basement of an elementary school. The confessional booth is a repurposed janitor's closet.

In the Catholic Church, the word indulgence has a different meaning.

Indulgences, once bought by rich people, were keys to absolution. Pay enough and your sins on this earth were forgiven forever, amen.

Later, the church and Lutherans put buying indulgences off limits, so rich people made charitable contributions instead.

Regular people could do good deeds or blister their fingers on rosaries to get a pass.

\\\\//

In Pittsburgh there's a church, St. Patrick's in the Strip District.

Pittsburgh's Strip District is an old-timey produce district with Wholey's fish market as one of its anchors. Wholey's famous giant fish is lit up in neon on the side of a warehouse. When developers threatened to take down the fish, the people of Pittsburgh rose up—petitions, protests—and the fish has prevailed for now.

These days, Pittsburgh's Strip District, a once practical place, now practical but also fancy, growing fancier by the day, consists of luxury condos and coffee shops. Enrico's Biscotti—made famous outside of Pittsburgh in Melissa Martin's beautiful film *A Wedding for Bella*, which Melissa Martin first called *The Bread, My Sweet*, a great title, the perfect title, but some marketing department chose *A Wedding for Bella* because weddings track well with target demographics, whatever—is still there. So is the Polish deli where you can buy blood sausage. Klavon's Ice Cream Shop, an old-time soda fountain where you can sit on stools that look like Coca-Cola bottle caps and buy penny candy that's still a penny, is for sale.

Okay, fine. The Strip—called the Strip because it's a narrow stretch, just one-half mile of land, between the Allegheny River and a mountain—also has a strip club. It's called Cheerleaders. I saw some strippers going to work once. They weren't dressed like cheerleaders, not a pom-pom in sight. They wore little tartan plaid skirts and white knee highs. They looked like Catholic school girls, but with boobs big and sturdy enough to rest school-lunch trays on.

Bless me. It's been decades since my last confession.

St. Patrick's—caddy-corner from Wholey's, whose fish looks like the Jesus fish children learn to draw in Bible school, one line, no beginning, no end, like the fish on my father's deathbed prayer book—is beautiful, a respite from the city, a respite from shopping.

St. Patrick's has a garden out front. The garden features statues of St. Patrick and the Virgin Mary, ivy-covered walls, lovely flowers all around, and benches where anyone who's tired can sit and rest a while. The church door and garden are never locked.

Inside St. Patrick's, which was built in 1808, are The Holy Stairs. The steps are replicas of the Church of the Holy Stairs at Scala Sancta in Rome. Only two other churches in the world contain them—the St. Anne de Beaupré shrine in Canada and the Shrine of Lourdes in France.

There are 28 steps in the Holy Stairs, the number of steps Christ in The Passion, his final period of life, took after Pontius Pilate washed his hands and sentenced death. The stairs are marble and unforgiving and go straight up. Believers climb these stairs on their knees. There is a sign at the base of the stairs that says, "Ascend on Knees – Only."

I have never climbed The Holy Stairs. Embarrassment, mostly, but also, even though I was raised Catholic, I am filled with doubt. Still, I have been to Rome, to the Vatican. The Holy Stairs in St. Patrick's Church in Pittsburgh feel like the most sacred of sacred ground.

Once when I was there, an old woman, maybe 70, maybe older, was ascending the stairs. I don't know if she believed in indulgences. I don't know what she prayed and hoped for as she lifted her black dress and put one bare arthritic knee, then another, onto the hard marble.

I hope whatever she prayed for and desired came to her.

This was years ago and I can still see her. Her white hair in a bun. A rosary clutched between her hands. Knee-high pantyhose. Black lace-up church shoes.

The effort. The climb.

There is a prayer: *Lord have mercy. Christ have mercy.*

One of my favorite songwriters, Mary Gauthier, has a song, "Mercy Now."

We all need that.

We need a little mercy now.

There is a book at the foot of The Holy Stairs where visitors can write prayers and notes to God. The book is beautiful and thick, filled with handwriting that goes back generations. There are messages about the dead, the lost, the broken. There are messages from people longing for love. There are many messages praying for people who are sick.

Cancer. Cancer.

Part of me wants to recount the messages written there, but those are private and not mine to share. If you're in Pittsburgh, you can read them. They will break your heart.

For now, listen to Mary Gauthier.

Whichever way you approach it, indulgence is a complicated thing. In theory, it offers amnesty from punishment in the afterlife. A plenary indulgence means a person's sin is brushed off like dandruff. A purgatorial indulgence just buys time. It shortens a sinner's sentence in Purgatory, that in-between place. How much time is shaved off varies—a year, five years—though no one has ever agreed on which clock governs the afterlife.

Also, forget about the bad place. No number of indulgences can get a soul a pass there.

Another catch: whatever your path to indulgence, you'll still have to confess first.

"Confessions have been down for years," the Rev. Tom Reese, former editor of the Catholic magazine *America*, says. "The church wants the idea of personal sin back in the equation."

There is another equation that limits how much anyone can get away with in this life. One indulgence per sinner per day.

Even the Catholic Church loses patience.

Thank you again for your patience, reader. Thank you for indulging me here.

The EPA declared the Westinghouse plant in Trafford, Pennsylvania a Superfund clean-up site in 1997. The EPA swooped in and did EPA things. Trafford was, supposedly, clear.

But in the 2000s, our little town got money to build soccer fields where the EPA clean-up happened. The contractors put down layers of concrete, many feet deep, to make the fields safe for children to play on.

The plant life around the soccer fields is oddly lush, a brilliant alien green. In his great book *Hiroshima*, John Hersey writes about the plant life that sprouted up after the atomic bomb. Some plants thrive on nuclear waste. Panic grass. Feverfew.

Both are abundant in my hometown.

Feverfew looks like fields of daisies, all those petals to wish on.

Panic grass looks like it's screaming.

My friends and I played on the site of the old Westinghouse factory, long before the EPA stepped in. In winter, the parking lot would freeze over, and we would ice skate and think how lucky we were to have such a glorious thing in our backyards.

"In service to mankind." That was Westinghouse's motto.

George Westinghouse was a good man. He would be heartbroken to think the site of one of his factories may have poisoned children.

He wanted people to make good wages, have nice sturdy homes, go to church, and not die before their time.

\ \ |

I live here still because home is home, because I somehow love this place, because I inherited this sturdy house from my mother when she died, after my father died—cancer, cancer—and my mother loved this house, and my father wanted me to live here forever.

Sometimes my father, like a proud realtor, would show me the copper pipes that ran along the ceiling of our basement. He'd point out the brickwork, the foundation, the ceramic tiles. He'd lean his full weight on the fireplace mantle.

"This isn't some cheap-ass shoebox," my father would say about the house he dreamt and helped build. "Everything here is made to last."

I told my parents I didn't want it—the house, the inheritance—and didn't think how much that probably hurt them. Still, when it came, I was grateful for it, because I had kids and little money and all these memories, and I couldn't (and can't) afford to move.

Some days I think I smell my father's cigarettes. Some days I reach for a salt shaker where it hasn't been for decades. Some days I try to sit on a chair that hasn't been there since my mother died and I nearly fall.

The mind knows things the body forgets.

The body knows things the mind forgets.

Sometimes I hear my mother's voice in our house.

The cigarette smoke is unfiltered. Pall Malls. My father's brand.

The weather reports for the Pittsburgh area in general, and my hometown in particular, feature a lot of coughing-emoji days, and so I care for my lungs, which are not the issue, but which are in the vicinity of my breasts, which are the problem now.

I care for my lungs because it's easy to consider cancer as a game of checkers, all jumps and king-mes. I go to a 24-hour gym once or twice a week and stroll on a treadmill.

At the gym, I watch Netflix or play *Words with Friends* while I stroll. I think *Words with Friends* helps ward off Alzheimer's more than weed does, though my husband believes in weed. I tell my husband, who I call Newman, who everyone calls Newman except for his parents who call him David or Dave, that word games are the thing.

"Justify it however you want," Newman says. "You're addicted to your phone."

"I'm addicted," I say, "to winning," and try to figure out how many points the word addicted could be worth.

"You really are an asshole," Newman says, but it sounds like "I love you."

I love him so much.

If you play the word "addicted" in *Words with Friends* and use all 7 letters, you'll earn 50 points.

Using all 7 letters in *Words with Friends* is also called a Bingo.

I manned the fish-fryer during bingo nights at the Trafford Polish Club from the time I was 12 until I went to college.

I worked for my grandmother, Ethel, who at 230 pounds ran the operation like a mob boss.

Ethel died when I was 21. She was just over 100 pounds when she died, her skin like a deflated balloon. Lung cancer, though she never smoked.

"Ain't that a kick in the fanny," Ethel said.

Pittsburgh people—so many of our sayings involve ass-kickings we didn't see coming.

"The world can really kick your ass," the character Roy Munson said in the movie *Kingpin*. "I only have a vague recollection of when it wasn't kicking mine."

The movie *Kingpin* was filmed in Trafford, at Lokay Lanes, our local bowling alley. Lokay Lanes still looks exactly like what you see in the movie—the same Lysol-ed bowling shoes, the same dank carpet, the same bowling balls, worn from years of kids and bowling leagues, the same vending machines with, maybe, the same flavored condoms for sale.

Cinnamon condoms? French ticklers? Are you serious, Lokay Lanes?

My son, and then my daughter, have had birthdays at Lokay Lanes. The people there are nice. The pizza is okay. Beer in the bar is cheap. The crane machines aren't rigged, so kids win on the regular. That's something.

In the movie *Kingpin*, Woody Harrelson plays Roy Munson. Woody Harrelson the actor once considered becoming a minister, but he put that on hold so he could enjoy his twenties and thirties.

"My eyes opened to the reality of the Bible being just a document to control people," Woody Harrelson told *Playboy*. "I started to discover the man-made nature of it."

My grandmother, Slovak I think, Ukrainian maybe, married to an Italian orphan, my grandfather, would use phrases I'd grow up thinking were English but weren't.

Her favorite: "Bozhe moi." My God.

I looked it up. It's Russian. Go figure.

My mother and her sisters always said they were Italian. They competed over meatballs. But me—adopted, Irish/German I think, didn't know anything. I love to cook. I love polkas and red wine. I believe in God or at least something bigger than this life, but I don't have words for what I am, beyond spiritual or agnostic and neither of those feels right.

"Be kind, babies," my dear Vonnegut said.

Maybe that's God and identity enough.

I make pretty good meatballs. I work a catering business with my best friend Syl, who is 100 percent Italian and lovely, with the best heart.

When I'm frustrated, I use the words I learned from my grandmother: "Bozhe moi." "Vaffanculo."

My God. Russian.

Fuck you. Italian.

My language, not my language. My heart. Not my heart.

My grandmother wasn't much for church.

"I should get a bathing suit," Ethel said, one of the last things I remember her saying. "A bikini, maybe," she said, and jiggled her belly. "Wouldn't that be something?"

Lately, Newman's been doing more research on marijuana and cancer cures. He works as a medical researcher. He's smart. He looks like an alcoholic ex-athlete who stocks shelves, but he's smart.

Over the past few weeks, he's been sending me links to articles and studies.

I haven't thought about how all this waiting has affected him. He doesn't seem scared, but maybe he is. I don't feel scared, but I think I am.

We stand in our bedroom. On both sides of our bed, there are towers of books, our mutual to-be-read piles. The towers go almost to the ceiling and lean menacingly over our heads as we sleep. I joke that one night the towers will collapse and we'll be smothered by all the books we didn't have time to read.

Newman hands me a mug of weed-laced lemonade. "It can't hurt," he says, and offers a puff off the vape pen he calls his Gandalf stick.

Newman has a long goatee. It's gray and black and red and wiry and makes him look wise, kind of Gandalf-ish in *Lord of the Rings.* Or like a Viking, or a peaceable biker, maybe.

When he's nervous or writing or thinking hard, Newman pulls his goatee into a point sharp enough to dip into ink. It uncurls at the bottom, like a question mark. He doesn't like me to mess with it, so of course I mess with it.

When I think of things I would miss most in this life, this is one of them.

The images that first gain access to your heart, Camus said.

My husband's sweet face.

I haven't seen his chin in twenty years, but I'm pretty sure it's lovely, too.

Newman gets his weed from a friend of a friend of a friend named something like Scoobie.

Scoobie procures his weed on the West Coast, then distills it in vodka. The drops come in pretty artisanal bottles, like essential oils. Scoobie's a gifted artist as well as a weed entrepreneur. His art looks a lot like Ralph Steadman's art. Steadman is the guy who illustrated Hunter S. Thompson's *Fear and Loathing in Las Vegas*, which seems right, though Hunter would have thought weed was for wimps, given his love for stronger drugs, acid and cocaine most of all.

Scoobie gives each weed strain its own name—*Afghani Pop Tart, Botswana Boogie, Grim Reaper.* Scoobie hand-draws the labels for each one, then colors them with crayons. Total artisanal, weed-farm-to-stoner-couch stuff. It's beautiful and amazing.

The illustration for *Grim Reaper* is a praying mantis with bulging red eyes.

Death has nothing on a praying mantis for scary.

A praying mantis, its front legs seemingly folded in peaceable prayer, can turn its head 180 degrees. It has two compound eyes and three other simple eyes, so it sees everything, always. The female mantis usually eats its mate after—or sometimes during—mating, with reflexes so fast they can't be seen by the naked human eye.

"Fun facts," my daughter Phelan, who loves nature documentaries, would say.

I've tried Scoobie's drops, but they make me nervous, the opposite of what they do for my husband, who gets horny and happy then drifts.

When Newman does a Scoobie drop, he sings in his sleep, a kind of prayer.

Newman makes a living as a social worker and a health scientist, but he's really a writer.

He writes songs as well as novels and books of poetry, and the songs he sings when he sleeps sound like truth.

Newman wrote a song for me once. The chorus goes like this: "We've had a lot of good years, with years to go."

I like to think when he sing-sleeps, this is the song he's singing.

Nature vs. nurture.

Forget I may have cancer.

Remember I'm adopted.

Is disease something we're born with and prone to, or the result of a life lived in a place that can make anyone sick?

Both, probably.

Either.

Neither.

When faced with mortality, the questions are always why and how and when, as if figuring out the answers makes any difference.

A praying mantis is known for its patience. It can hold still and wait. And wait.

And wait.

Not unlike cancer, when you think about it.

"An expert at ambush," *National Geographic* says about mantises.

"This world is not a perfect system" is my go-to answer for my children when they want to know why friends turn awful, or why people are mean, or why people suffer and die, or why nothing seems fair, including everything.

I want a better life for my children, but this is the world we have been gifted, if gifted is the right word.

Most days I think it is.

Most days I think of this life as a gift.

"Tell me," my beloved poet Mary Oliver said, "what is it you plan to do with your one wild and precious life?"

As a kid, I wanted to see Paris, Vienna. I wanted to see the Northern Lights. I wanted New York and Madrid and love, most of all. That.

I have seen Paris, Vienna, the Northern Lights. I lived in New York. I spent months in Madrid. Once I stopped moving, I found love.

Most of all, that.

With my one wild, precious, middle-aged life, I'd just like to stick around a while. Read some of those books, maybe.

I'd like to have enough time to be patient.

I'd like to play it as it lays.

The highest-scoring word in both *Word with Friends* and old-school *Scrabble* is *oxyphenbutazone.*

Oxyphenbutazone will, if played in a perfect moment, score you 1,778 points in *Scrabble* and 1,674 points in *Words with Friends.*

Oxyphenbutazone was the name of a bad and obsolete medication—an anti-inflammatory that suppressed white-blood-cell production. It was basically chemotherapy before chemotherapy.

I don't think *Oxyphenbutazone* ever saved anyone.

I would love to find a word that would save everyone.

How many points would a word like that be worth?

Lynyrd Skynyrd and the Expanding Universe of Vowels

Chapter 2

When the oncology nurse calls, I assume she's going to tell me I'm fine, no worries, and I should go on making healthy choices, good day, goodbye.

I've already laid off red meat. I'm doing yoga on the daily, and when my husband hands me a vape pen filled with weed, I put up one hand like a traffic cop.

"It wards off Alzheimer's," he says.

"Too late," I say. "Who are you again?"

I've cut back on coffee and given up Red Bull as some odd penance.

"Red Bull gives people strokes," I say to my husband when I catch him chugging a large cranberry one.

"But good strokes. The kind you stay awake for," he says, and goes on chugging.

"I remember a time before energy drinks," I say, all wistful-like.

Phelan says, "You were born in the 1900s," which sounds wrong, too old, then not, just the right age.

"We used to do this thing called sleep," I say.

Phelan says, "Okay Boomer," and giggles.

"Gen X," I say, a little tender about my age and generational stereotypes. "Have you ever seen *The Breakfast Club*?"

Phelan says, "Was that something you did before school way back when?"

My daughter was born in 2004. She knows Winona Ryder from the series *Stranger Things*. She thinks Johnny Depp's *Wino* tattoo is because he has a drinking problem, who knows, not judging.

Stranger Things is set in the 1980s. The kids in the show ride bikes with banana seats and handlebar tassels, just like the bikes I knew growing up. This makes me feel younger, immortal maybe, the same way I feel whenever I hear Lynyrd Skynyrd's "Freebird" or Led Zeppelin's "Stairway to Heaven," which the radio stations here in Pittsburgh have been playing on repeat since forever, perpetual time machines.

"Did you eat eggs and talk about current events?" Phelan wants to know about *The Breakfast Club*. "Did you love toast?"

Fuck you, Phelan, my beautiful daughter. I love you so much.

I remember a time when breakfast detention was a serious thing, though I was straight-edged and had to do time only once.

I got caught selling oregano in a baggie to a girl in prep school who thought the oregano was some premium weed and made everyone call her Robert Plant because Led Zeppelin.

But that's another story.

Robert Plant would know the difference between oregano and premium weed. Just saying.

We were talking about time.

In the 1900s, before energy drinks, we had coffee and NoDoz pills and diet pills and naps. Kids who couldn't get premium weed would sometimes smoke banana peels, but that just gave them headaches.

I remember a time before schools were on the news, before *shelter in place* was a thing, before automatic weapons and metal detectors, before English teachers turned in students who wrote essays about madness, before anyone worried about active shooters or anything other than mean girls and bullies and what was in the mystery meat the cafeteria passed off as hamburgers, and where we'd sit on the bus, and who drew the dicks on the buses' metal seat backs, and who was the artist who remembered to put wiry hairs on all the ball sacs, that attention to detail, genius really, but I don't tell my daughter any of this.

About *The Breakfast Club* I say, "We should watch it together."

I say, "I'll make popcorn."

Phelan says, "Okay, maybe," like she'll have her people call my people to maybe set a date somewhere around never.

These days my daughter is still kissing me on the top of my head, the way I kissed her when she was younger, a kiss that says there-there, a kiss that says, "I love you," a kiss that says, "Oh, sweetie, the things you don't know."

Some days I switch on WDVE, which is the most classic of classic Pittsburgh radio stations, and I'm back in the 1980s, which were the 1900s, nearly prehistoric in my daughter's lovely mind.

When I listen to 'DVE—no one in Pittsburgh uses the W, kind of like in New York when tourists pronounce Houston Street the same as that place in Texas and get spontaneously mugged—I'm back at Ardmore Roller Rink, All Skate, figure eights, backwards, forwards, pink pom-poms on my skates, disco lights flashing, the smell of burnt pizza and Super Pretzels and teenage sweat, all moldy grapefruit and Love's Baby Soft, the snake-slither of a pink satin jacket over my arms, my long hair crimped and teased and Aqua Netted big enough to have its own zip code, a strange boy's raspberry-Icee'd tongue in my mouth, Ladies' Choice, everything possible, *free as a bird now.*

How can life seem so long and short all at once?

Einstein could explain it, maybe, but he's been dead a long time.

First Ardmore Roller Rink became a gym, then a realty office, then nothing. It sits vacant, the empty basement of a brown-bricked bank building.

"Time is a construct," I say to my daughter, who rolls her lovely eyes.

Einstein died of an aneurysm in Spring, 1955. He refused a surgery that maybe could have saved him, saying: "I want to go when I want. It is tasteless to prolong life artificially. I have done my share; it is time to go. I will do it elegantly."

Grace under pressure, Hemingway would say.

After his death, pieces of Einstein's brain ended up in mason jars. Thomas Stoltz Harvey, the man who conducted Einstein's autopsy, drove the brain-bits around in the trunk of his car for years until he was discovered doing so in 1978.

Einstein's brain had traveled across many states and into Canada.

"Life is like riding a bicycle," Einstein once said. "To keep your balance, you must keep moving."

I never wondered until this moment why Lynyrd Skynyrd's name is spelled like that.

I know the band took its name as a joke about Leonard Skinner, a gym teacher who hated long-haired boys.

But why all the Ys?

Marketing, probably.

Weed, definitely.

Something for kids to ponder while staring at album covers and smoking in their parents' basement.

Remember album covers?

If you're from the 1900s, you do.

I studied those covers.

I loved Led Zeppelin's "Zoso," an old man carrying a bundle of twigs, the meaning of which no one has ever fully deciphered. I loved all those humans hidden in the lion on the cover of Santana's debut album. I loved the sweet faces of Lynyrd Skynyrd on the album that spelled their band name phonetically, those long-haired hippie freaks, the horror of gym teachers everywhere, those babies—Ronnie Van Zant, and later Steve Gaines, Cassie Gaines—who would be dead before I could love their music like I would later in life when I quit trying to be cool.

I'm feeling philosophical these days, which is something that happens, maybe, when facing what could be a dire diagnosis about a disease that has become as common as acne.

"The goal of all art is to gain access to the one or two images that first gained access to our hearts," said Camus, who I've referenced on repeat, who we should all read and re-read.

All those album covers.

Remember?

Remember?

"When you're dead, you're a dead pecker-head," dear John Prine used to say, but he was quoting his father.

John Prine's album covers were often just a picture of John Prine, looking earnest and eternal in jeans and a work shirt.

John Prine thought his father was wrong about death. In one song, John Prine plans a party in the afterlife where he gets to say told-you-so to his dad.

I like that.

Indulge me, please.

We'll have fun in the afterlife together.

You, John Prine, and me and everyone we've ever loved.

Newman says some people believe weed not only wards off dementia but could also cure cancer.

Fuck dementia. Let's deal with the thing at hand.

My husband is a practical man. He loves me nonetheless.

I don't know this yet, but a few months from now, after some surgeries, whatever, when I have to sleep in a medical recliner because a bed won't do, because a bed will cause pain, my husband will take a single mattress from our son's bunk bed and place it by my side. The mattress will still be covered in Spiderman sheets, faded in the places where my sleeping son used to lie.

Newman, built like the football player he was, will sleep on the floor on this tiny Spiderman mattress for weeks. He'll reach up to hold my hand and his bad shoulder will lock up because he won't let go.

But that comes later.

For now, Newman keeps doing research. He keeps reading medical journals. He has two master's degrees to my one, and seven books to my six. Not that it's a competition. I'm establishing him as a trusted source and trust for me is no easy thing.

I'm adopted. I don't believe in people, though I love so many of them. I believe in my husband and love him. We've been married almost 20 years, but I want more.

Eternity. What an amazing word, the way it stretches the mouth, expanding like a universe of vowels and consonants. Eternity.

In *Words with Friends*, the word Eternity is also a bingo. All seven letters, plus one.

Seven, that angel number, all mysticism and perfection. In the Bible, seven is the number of God's creation, perfection, the number of days in the week.

The seventh day, Sabbath, the day of rest.

Eternity is worth 50-plus points in *Words with Friends.*

How many points are enough for a lifetime?

How many years are enough for a lifetime?

Whatever freedom used to mean to me, now I want the opposite. Grounding. Family. Love. Sex.

"Sit on my face," Newman says at least three times a week.

Sorry if that sounds crass but being married for so long and having someone love you like that seems worth testimony.

When I do dishes, Newman sneaks up behind me and humps my ass. When I sleep naked because mid-life hot flashes make my blood turn to lava, he strokes my thighs. Twenty years in, my husband still makes me feel beautiful and desired to the point where I need to tell him to knock it off.

When I am very sick, he will reach up from his tiny mattress and hold my hand for weeks, months. The Spiderman mattress will meld from the imprint of my son's tiny body to my husband's body.

Set us free from this mortal coil, someone said. William Blake, maybe.

No thank you.

I'm good.

"I'm sorry," the oncology nurse on the phone says.

She'll repeat it, again, again, her words skipping like a scratched record, a hiccup.

I love her.

I hate her.

She feels like a passenger on one of my flights, a blip, a sweetness, something else.

Saturday Night Live had a segment once called "Total Bastard Airlines." Helen Hunt and David Spade made the airline "bah-bye" famous.

David Spade, that sweetheart, was on my flight once. It had been a hard day, I don't remember why, but there were a lot of hard days. David Spade cheered me up by helping me de-plane when we landed.

De-plane. What a word.

David Spade stood at the door with me and sent passengers off. He said, "Bah-bye," and "Which part didn't you understand?" and "Bah-bye now."

He said, "Knock knock."

He said, "Who's there?

He said, "Bah-bye now."

David Spade, you sweet funny beautiful human. Thank you for the memory. Thank you for the light. Delight.

De-Light.

See what I did there?

Sometimes on flights sans David Spade, I played with words a little, like I do now.

"Apple pie," I'd say as passengers de-planed. "Apple pie now."

In all my years of flying the only people who ever caught on were kids and this one old lady, a beauty who, during a particularly rough flight, shouted with joy mid-turbulence, "They should charge extra for this!" while everyone around her gripped their armrests, prayed, or hyperventilated into airsick bags, certain we'd crash.

The thing about airplanes: a lot of things happen that feel like the end, but planes rarely crash. When they do, it's awful of course, but most of the time, it's fine. We're fine.

Cancer isn't the death sentence it used to be. I try to remember that.

The lovely old lady on my flight kept calling me nurse.

"Oh nurse! You're a good one," she said whenever I brought her juice and snacks.

Apple pie. Bah-bye. Apple pie now.

Get it? Funny, right?

/ / \

The nurse on the phone?

Later I will have to ask her to repeat many things. I will exhaust her patience because of how little I've paid attention. An appointment for another biopsy. No, it can't wait. Yes, sooner is better.

Later I will have to write things down and ask for clarifications. I will replay the words again and again before I can begin to understand.

\ \ /

Back in the 1900s, there was a show called *Fantasy Island* that made the phrase de-plane famous before it meant anything in airline-speak.

Ricardo Montalbán, the star, described *Fantasy Island* as TV's version of Purgatory.

Montalbán's character, Mr. Roarke, had the power to fulfill people's fantasies, often to nightmarish ends, since the people who ended up on *Fantasy Island* were more or less shitheads who deserved whatever they had coming.

Hervé Villechaize played Tattoo, Mr. Roarke's diminutive assistant.

Montalbán saw his character Mr. Roarke as a fallen angel in charge. He called Tattoo his little cherub. Hervé Villechaize, a little person who preferred the word midget, became famous for shouting his catchphrase at the beginning of every episode of *Fantasy Island.*

"The plane! The plane!"

Later in life, people would stop Hervé Villechaize on the street. They would come up to him in restaurants. They'd post up outside his home and beg him to say it, say it.

Hervé Villechaize, born in France, an acclaimed painter before he became an actor, had a bit of an accent. "The plane! The plane!" sounded like "De-plane! De-plane!"

Before he landed on *Fantasy Island*, Hervé Villechaize played an evil henchman named Nick Nack in a James Bond movie. Before that, he worked as a rat-catcher's assistant in South Central Los Angeles. Later, he can be seen as the legs of Oscar the Grouch on *Sesame Street*, such is the life of a little person in Hollywood.

We all do whatever it takes to get by in this life.

On "That Teen Show" in 1983, Hervé Villechaize, bullied as a child, troubled as an adult, fired from *Fantasy Island* over salary demands and bad behavior, said he'd finally learned to love life. Ten years later, Hervé Villechaize shot and killed himself. He'd become very sick and was in pain. His lungs were too small. Other organs, including his heart, were too big.

"He thought of himself as a proud mustang, but he'd become a carousel pony," his wife, Kathy Self, said.

Hervé Villechaize recorded his own death, including his final words, on a tape recorder he hid in a potted plant. On the recording, he says, "I just have to do this, and everything will be fine." After he pulls the trigger and doesn't die, he says, "Whoa. Well, I guess I just have to wait."

Hervé Villechaize was 50.

"I just want everyone to know I love them," Hervé Villechaize said.

Ricardo Montalbán went on to have a career that spanned seven decades, *Star Trek: Wrath of Khan*, etc. But Ricardo Montalbán is also famous for commercials he did for the Chrysler Cordoba, where he touted the luxury of the car's fine Corinthian leather.

There is no such thing as fine Corinthian leather.

The leather for the Chrysler Cordoba came from New Jersey.

Before he died, Hervé Villechaize starred in an ad for Dunkin' Donuts' mini donuts, where he said "Da plain! Da plain!" and pointed to the donuts he wanted.

In his last note to his wife, Hervé Villechaize wrote, "Your love made me feel like a giant. That's how I want you to remember me."

About Skynyrd, a band he loves, Newman says, "They were probably high and someone figured, hey, Ys are cool. Plus, it might have kept them from being sued by their gym teacher, Leonard."

Imagine Leonard, a whistle around his rubbery sun-pocked neck, running kids around a track, ordering the long hairs to drop and give him 20, or worse.

Leonard in boxer shorts and a stained t-shirt.

Leonard retired in his dank basement.

Leonard smelling of boiled hotdogs.

Leonard scratching his withered nuts.

Leonard listening to Lynyrd Skynyrd on the radio, those long-hairs making millions.

Leonard, considering how little he knew about anything,

Leonard, who maybe wondered if he wasted his one and only life.

Jokes About Needles Probably Aren't Funny

Chapter 3

For the biopsy my doctor ordered, I am clad in a pink hospital gown, strapped into a chair and wheeled to a machine designed to press my breast into a flesh panini, then stick it full of needles, which, lidocaine or no lidocaine, I feel.

The pain is so intense I would gnaw my own breast off with my teeth to never feel such pain again.

"I don't think it's working," I say to the nurses, meaning the lidocaine, meaning *help*, meaning *stop*, meaning *please.*

"My hand is here if you need it," one kind nurse says.

I'm embarrassed by how much I need it.

I hold onto this lovely stranger like her hand is the only thing tethering me to my body.

"Try not to look," she says, though my eyes are already shut. Behind my eyelids, the needles I imagine are, maybe, worse.

Years ago, Newman and I took our Locklin to a superhero movie. There was a scene with a huge machine, a lot of needles. A character wanted power, immortality, and he allowed himself to be strapped to a table. Many needles came down, all loaded with super medicine. The character, an ordinary human, turned into something called Abomination.

"I'm out," my son said, and bolted for the exit.

He was six. Probably not great parenting, in retrospect, but still.

He's been terrified of doctors and needles ever since.

Abomination. What a word.

This machine I'm not looking at—I don't know how it would seem in a movie, but I'm pretty sure it's terrifying. The sound alone is otherworldly, hydraulic. My mouth tastes metallic. Everything smells too clean, all rubbing alcohol and bleach and ether.

"Don't look," another nurse says as I go on squeezing the first nurse's hand.

"Just relax," one of the techs says.

There are only two techs in the room, both men. I love men, but their presence here seems off, the focus being breasts and all. The techs seem intent on the machinery, their voices farther away, disembodied. I'm sure if I opened my eyes, I'd see that they're kind, too, but I keep my eyes closed. I squeeze the hand of the nurse, who I love so much in this moment I want to weep, and maybe I do a little, I'm not sure.

"You need to hold still," one of the men says. He sounds annoyed but professional.

The other makes his voice soft. "Try not to move. Just breathe."

I want to say, "But breathing means moving."

I want to say, "I'm trying. I am."

I want to be tough and kind, funny enough to make the techs and nurses like me, because if they like me even a little, they might be gentle. I want to tell them how I didn't cry, not once, when I was in labor with my son, then my daughter. I want them to know that I'm a reasonable person, smart, mostly unflappable—that this moment is an exception.

I want to say *please* and *I'm sorry* and *my mother was a nurse* and *I want to be a good patient, the best patient, I know how, please, if I could have a minute, please, sorry sorry.*

The pain is so bad it seems unbearable, though I know so many unbearable things in the end are bearable. I want to believe the techs are trying for gentle. I am trying to love them the way I love the nurses.

The nurses keep talking.

"I know it's hard."

"You're doing great."

"Let me know if you feel woozy."

The nurse with her hand in mine tells me a story—how she's afraid to drive ever since her accident. She was seven months pregnant with her daughter. She had to be pulled from her car, cut from the steel. Her daughter is fine now, four years old. The nurse is fine now. A survivor.

"I feel it every time I get in a car," she says, about terror. "It's something you can't get over, maybe."

She says, "I don't want to pass my fear to my daughter."

She says, "We pass our fears on, maybe, no matter what," which is true and serious, but she laughs, and her laughter sounds like fluttering birds.

"We need to go in again," one tech says, as if he's drilling for fissures in rock.

I want to say *no, please.*

I think I don't say anything.

I hope I don't say anything.

I want to be a good patient, the best patient. My mom, the nurse. All that.

I try breathing. Five-count breaths. Deep inhales, deep exhales. The men ask me about my children, their ages, and I answer. Seventeen. Fourteen. Son. Daughter.

Yes, I am looking forward to their futures.

Yes, I am their mother—a reason to go through this, a reason to hold still and be good.

My son is graduating from high school later today, yes.

Yes, I am glad I will see that.

Yes, I am proud.

I think of my son, in his green graduation gown, singing his alma mater, which was my alma mater long ago: *"Years from now we will all recall fond memories of these days."*

I think of my son running for the theater exit, all those needles coming down, *abomination.*

"Try to think of this like a champagne cork popping," one tech says as more needles—many needles maybe, *so* many needles—press down again, again.

I keep my eyes closed.

I try not to see or count the needles in my mind.

The pressure feels like my nipple popping off, a party prop, something that should spew confetti but feels like it's spewing blood.

"Be still now," a tech says.

I open my eyes, but it doesn't matter. The room shrinks, like a camera lens closing. I think about party poppers, the confetti I vacuumed up, the confetti that kept showing up weeks or years after birthdays, and now my son's graduation. So much life left to celebrate.

Yes, I want to be healthy.

Yes, I'd like many years with my children.

Yes, I say, over and over.

"I'm not sure the lidocaine is working," I say again, and my voice sounds lucid but far away, not mine.

"We gave you two shots," one tech says. "You shouldn't feel a thing."

"Hang in there, mom," says the other.

I try.

I do.

When the procedure is over, the nurses wheel me away from the machine. They loosen the straps, the sound of Velcro tearing.

I think I thank them. I think I tell them to have a good day.

I don't feel a thing when I collapse, though I remember promising the techs and nurses I wouldn't drop on them.

Before the room goes dark, I think I make an Abomination joke: "Amomination … Get it? A mom."

Probably not funny.

I think I apologize.

For the joke, for being so much trouble, for causing a fuss.

I hope I do.

"Grace under pressure." Hemingway, my touchstone.

I want a little grace. I want to be graceful.

I want to hold onto whatever dignity I have left, exposed as I am in this pink hospital gown, in front of these strangers who've seen what no one in my family has seen—how afraid I am, how weak, how human.

Postscript

Excerpts From the *Washington Post* Comments Section
and One Five-Page Handwritten Letter Sent to My Home
in Response to the Previous Chapter Entitled "Jokes About Needles Probably Aren't Funny"

Letter Dated October 31, 2021 from Dr. XXX:
Writing or talking about this scares people. Women will put off having this procedure that can save lives. Many women will read this and vow never to consent to a breast biopsy. Please consider this.

Comment/blunoser
Beautiful. I'm terrified for when my pain-time comes and no one listens. I will find your essay in my mind for comfort.

Comment/60somethingCH
I had a similar experience with the needles, which were inserted just before my lumpectomy. My body tried to faint from pain, but I fought through it. Good thing. If I had fainted, the doctor later told me, they'd have to start over.

Comment/Lynn4567
This is the first time I have heard someone go through the pain I also endured when I had a core biopsy on my breast. I too, cried with the pain. Lidocaine was definitely not enough to help. The doctor told me he couldn't continue if I didn't stop. I wished I was under anesthesia. It was malignant and 6 cm and had spread. But that was 8 years ago, and that pain is what I remember most, above surgery, chemo and radiation.

Comment/dthb0150
As a BC survivor, I am outraged women are still being tortured this way.

Comment/Powered by Plants
I had a lumpectomy, expecting incredible pain—but it was far less painful, even afterward. In fact, I was still bruised from the biopsy, but not bruised at all from the surgery. Why is that the case?

Comment/suesos
I have had a "needle loc." Fish were hooks inserted in my breast near the chest wall and then my breast was compressed. They were left in place so the surgeon could see where to biopsy. I screamed so much the surgeon threatened not to do my surgery unless I could stop crying.

Comment/Powered by Plants
Maybe radiologists are sadists? I had a wire inserted before my lumpectomy. When I complained about the pain, the radiologist chided me that it was "just for a little while, nothing undue, certainly bearable."

Comment/suesos
This is a barbaric procedure. I can't believe they are still doing it. Lidocaine was not used because they said it would distort the X-ray. It was hideous to listen to the nurses and doctor telling me that "most

people" don't find it that painful. I would have rather been told up front that it might be the worst pain ever, but that it might save my life and that screaming is a natural reaction.

Comment/Bronzer to Rikers
I have friends who lived in the Soviet Union. Dental procedures were routinely done without pain relief. One of my friends had a root canal without pain relief. So if you ever meet an older person from the former USSR who is missing teeth, have sympathy for them.

Comment/MikeFromEnderby
Lidocaine stopped working on me during dental procedures. The dentist would pump so much into me that my heart would race for minutes. The pain was intense. Then I went to a specialist for implants and he used Ultracaine. It was heaven for three implants, then it stopped working for the fourth implant. On a pain scale of 1 to 10, that exceeded a 12

Comment/Visibly
Been there, done that!

Comment/NW Luna
Perhaps those clinicians should get biopsies on their testicles with insufficient pain relief to see how it feels.

Comment/JohnnyBoy6061
Wow. It truly doesn't sound like you "love men." Your writing speaks volumes about your mindset. Your ordeal would probably have been much more bearable if only you could have shed your prejudices. Sad.

Comment/seaduck2001
Why so threatened JohnnyBoy6061?

Comment/JohnnyBoy6061
She sounds quite overwrought, indeed hysterical. Poor thing!

Comment/washjeff
I'd call you words WAPO wouldn't allow.
But you get the drift, Johnny.

Comment/sfbiker
The doctor that did my prostate biopsy was male, but the three assistants (not sure if they were all nurses) were all female and I didn't question why any of them were there even though none of them have a prostate.

Comment/Quintessential
As a man, you have that luxury. Men aren't routinely harassed and assaulted by female health care workers. Women are harassed and assaulted by male health care workers and have been for a long time.

The fact that the writer even feels like she needs to say, "I love men" is proof of how abused women are and how we feel like we have to qualify all of our criticisms concerning men with "but but but I love men really," lest we be attacked.

There should only be women involved in situations like this and it's an outrage that men were there. Women should NEVER be subjected to that when they're at their most vulnerable and terrified.

Comment/Brent Leatherman
Yeah, us old white guys are the cause of every problem in the world, so we've been assured by people like you, ad nauseam. Go ahead and fix it yourself. You've lost an ally. You're on your own.

Comment/dc_native1
It's clear you are not and never have been an ally of women. So no loss.

Comment/sfbiker
I don't know if you've ever had someone stick a probe up your butt with the intent to shoot needles through your rectal wall in your prostate, but that's a pretty vulnerable position. And I never once thought that the women in the room were unworthy or incapable of assisting with the procedure.

Comment/seaduck2001
No way I'd have a man doing my mammogram let alone a procedure like this.

Comment/Quacker
Quintessential.

Comment/60somethingCH
Thinking of your kids probably saved your life.

Comment/Kathleen Miller
WHY would you take a SIX YEAR OLD to that kind of movie?!!!? way to go... i have the same question for my own daughter and her husband... they LOVED those movies when they were kids! which a little math shows to have been teen years... so now their house at bedtime is like an airport runway... bright lights in every room and hallway.
Way to go.

Comment/WonderingWanderer
People weren't expecting that. This is what IMDB put into their parental guide about that scene: "Blonsky gets shots of the Serum in

the back. He is shown to be experiencing lots of pain." That's it. The scene caught a lot of people off guard.

...so now their house at bedtime is like an airport runway... bright lights in every room and hallway.

Wait, did you know the movie being referenced was *The Incredible Hulk* and not some slasher film?

Letter Dated October 31, 2021 from Dr. X:
Please stop scaring people.

I See You, Beauty

Chapter 4

At the Panera in Westmoreland Mall, the sun gleams through the huge windows and the chairs are padded and more comfortable than the ones at the moody coffee shop I usually frequent.

I've gone to this mall to work, which for me means write. I've gone to this mall because I'm one of those writers who likes public spaces. Writing is a lonely business. The static of strangers sipping coffee and chatting makes it seem less so.

When he wasn't standing sullen at his typewriter, Hemingway, the writer I love most, wrote in bars and cafes.

"I see you, beauty, and you are mine," Hemingway wrote about a young woman he saw in a café in Paris. He meant there, in that public space, he could take the world in, like light, like air. He meant nothing and no one was ever lost to him. He meant the universe provides. He meant, through art, through writing, we all live forever knowing we will die.

Many people misread Hemingway. They call him a misogynist or worse. They flag this passage in *A Moveable Feast* as an example of "lookism," as if every writer and artist were not guilty of loving and absorbing and preserving the beauty of the world.

"I see you, beauty," Hemingway wrote in that cafe in Paris, which is not so unlike a Panera in a shopping mall in Greensburg, Pennsylvania.

Beauty is everywhere if you're open to it.

Through art, beauty and every living thing can last forever.

In art, everyone and everything we've ever loved will never die.

Through art, we accept that everyone and everything we've ever loved will die.

All these things are true.

Okay, so PETA is not a Hemingway fan and for good reason, all that bullfighting and big-game hunting and posing, but I love Hemingway's clarity, his belief in the possibility of one true sentence, his tragic longing for his first wife Hadley.

If you want to read a love story, read *Hemingway in Love* by Hemingway's best friend, A.E. Hotchner.

Do not ever read the restored version of *A Moveable Feast.* The original is what Hemingway intended. Editing great writers after they're dead is the worst. Restored = marketing. Marketing is a necessary aberration, but not at the expense of art.

Hemingway, alive, also loved booze, of course, and cats. All of his cats were polydactyls. Their descendants, with all their extra toes, are still there, at his house in Key West.

You can pet them if you'd like.

Hemingway, like Emily Dickinson, loved dogs, too. Hemingway named his dog Black Dog, remember? While people often came up short, Black Dog never left Hemingway's side. Black Dog, scholars say, is a metaphor for depression. The heaviness of that. Black dog, my father's dream said, carried the yellow cat of a soul to the next life.

But Black Dog was a real dog, and Hemingway's loss was no dream or metaphor.

In that dream my father had, my father was the yellow cat.

"What the hell do you make of that?" my father said.

My father had lost all his hair from radiation and chemo the summer he started to lose everything. I've told you this, but maybe it's worth repeating.

A yellow cat, according to dream experts that were not in my father's *Success Dream Book*, means you cannot win against the forces against you. A black dog in a dream symbolizes death, which is pretty obvious, Prof. De Herbert.

My father had a hard time in this life. If losing him didn't hurt so much, I'd be glad in the end my father found a way through, a black dog to carry him to whatever waited.

I hope that side is real and better, don't you?

I hope John Prine's father was wrong.

Remember that song? Remember that death? No one wants to end up a dead pecker-head.

"It hurts. It hurts," Hervé Villechaize said about life.

"I'll save you," my son Locklin, the Human Spider, said.

I wish the other side of this life painless and beautiful. I wish it magic, a golden doorway to a world where gravity doesn't rule and we can save one other.

Sometimes my father comes to me in my dreams. He does cartwheels, something he never did in this life.

In my dreams, he's doing cartwheels to make me happy. In my dreams, my father sometimes builds me a desk.

"For your writing," he says.

He says, "Are you happy, sweetheart, or what?"

Sometimes in dreams I take my father's face in my hands, something I would have never done in this life, and he is young and beautiful, and I say to whomever else shows up in the dream, "Can you see him? Can you see?"

When I wake, my pillow is wet with the tears I'm free to let loose in my sleep.

If there is another life, I hope my father found the happiness this world denied him.

In my dreams, my father's smiling, a pack of Pall Malls tucked into the chest pocket of his pink dress shirt, his legs and arms spiraling an X, all those cartwheels that go on and on.

PETA, those right-meaning fascists, should give Hemingway a pass.

He loved Black Dog.

Hemingway, who passed himself off as a big-game hunter, had so much tenderness for tiny creatures—cats, Black Dog, us.

I loved my father.

"The only thing that can ruin a good day is people," Hemingway wrote in *A Moveable Feast,* his long love letter to his first wife Hadley and to Paris.

Hemingway loved Hadley and Paris, maybe most of all.

Holding onto the things we love most in this life holds us to this life.

I believe this.

It's why I'm telling you about everything I love.

I want to live. I know that's fleeting. So maybe this time capsule will do.

What do you want? What things do you love? What moments will you keep?

Tell me, please. I'll hold them with my own.

Okay, so the Westmoreland Mall in Greensburg, Pennsylvania, is not Paris. Though maybe, when you live in Paris, Paris is not the Paris of dreams.

To think of Paris as ordinary, to become weary of all those lights and good wine and cheese and the Louvre—I should consider this.

The Mona Lisa is tiny. Imagine that.

I was shocked to see it, *The Mona Lisa* being so huge in my mind, the epitome of eternal art. It's the size of two loaves of bread. It's the size of two shoe boxes, such ordinary things.

I'm also writing at the mall because I have a hard time writing at home.

I've been slacking. I'm often slacking. I'll use pretty much any excuse to avoid writing because writing is hard.

At home, there are dishes and dust and a carpet that needs cleaning and a toilet that needs scrubbing and socks that need matching and multiple Netflix series about Ted Bundy and Jeffrey Dahmer and other serial killers I'd like to write about but don't because I'm not true-crime-gifted like that, though I'm addicted to their horrible stories. They remind me of mortality, maybe. Writers can't do much about our own obsessions, which become our subjects, which become our lives.

My life is my family and work, things everybody deals with, but few want to binge-watch.

"Why don't you write one of those Stephen King books?" my father used to say, but my father's been dead for many years now.

\/\

My father, the steelworker, machinist, laborer, cut a record once.

When I said he gave up singing, it meant more than I can imagine.

For a minute, my father was the golden voice of Braddock, Pennsylvania, the next Bobby Vinton, the Polish Prince, the next Perry Como. Streets in Canonsburg, Pennsylvania, are named for Bobby Vinton and Perry Como. Bobby Vinton Boulevard, Perry Como Way.

The house my father grew up in on Cherry Way in Braddock looks like a busted tooth, the windows boarded up, gang tags spray-painted red over the boards.

One of the tags reads, *What.*

Another of the tags reads, *Fuck it.*

Another tag reads, *Nah,* like the place isn't worth being fucked.

The Mona Lisa has been attacked a handful of times. A rock, a teacup, and most recently, one assault by pastry. French.

The most serious—red spray paint.

Another of the tags on my father's house reads, *DEMO.* Red spray paint.

The Mona Lisa is behind bulletproof, pastry-proof glass.

She's fine.

Perry Como was a singer, but he wanted to be the best barber in Canonsburg. My father wanted to be a singer, but he gave up singing for a war, then the mills.

"You can't live in a dream world," my father said to me, but more to himself about the life choices that made him mostly miserable, though choice is the wrong word.

Choice is a privilege.

Choice is something handed down from the suffering of others.

My father gave me a life full of choices.

My father paid my rent in college. He sent money for groceries and books.

I don't mean he was rich. I mean he gave me whatever he could so I could worry less, though I worried constantly.

I had a nervous breakdown my senior year. A terrible break-up, heartache I thought would never pass. I latched on to F. Scott Fitzgerald. I'd read *The Crack-Up* in a literature class, and it seemed to sum up what I was feeling and not feeling.

"I had weaned myself from all the things I used to love," Fitzgerald wrote. "I slept on the heart side now because I knew that the sooner I could tire that out, even a little, the sooner would come that blessed hour of nightmare which, like a catharsis, would enable me to better meet the new day."

I stayed in bed for days at a time. I stopped eating. I showered sporadically. My poor sweet roommates worried. They worried in ways no one in their twenties should ever have to worry about another person living in their space. I took up too much space. I took up too much time.

I'm sorry.

I'm sorry.

My roommates would bring the phone to my bedside when my father called. He'd say, "Are you eating okay?"

He'd say, "What do you need? Tell me."

He'd say, "I love you, you know that."

He'd say, like he always said, "Are you happy, sweetheart, or what?"

Now, in my 50s, I'd tell my father yes, I'm happy. I'd say, yes, I lived.

I'd thank him for my life. I'd say I need him. I'd say I didn't know how much.

But I talk to my father on the page more than I ever talked to him in life.

When my father was alive, he tried to drown me to show me drowning.

I was a child. I had one swimming lesson, at the YMCA in Wilmerding, Pennsylvania. I came home and told my parents I could swim.

My father, angry for reasons I didn't understand, took me to a public pool. He took me to the deep end and pushed me in.

I haven't forgotten.

Love and fear. Fear and love.

I felt the water close in around me, the weight of that. In my memory, all I see is blue and the thick rope of my father's arm coming down like a god, lifting me up. How I gasped for air. How the sky seemed to open.

How I hated my father then. How I loved him.

My father wanted to keep me safe and so he showed me fear. He wanted to keep me from drowning and so he showed me drowning.

"Stop scaring people," the doctor who wrote that letter about my biopsy story said. He meant well, but terror has its own power.

May all of us live forever. May all of us understand how fleeting this life is, how fragile.

"Are you happy, sweetheart?" my unhappy father asked me again and again.

"Are you happy, beauties, or what?" I say to my children and pull them close.

"That will show you, jackass," my father said as he wrapped me in a towel and shuffled me off into the car, back home.

My son's first movie was *Charlotte's Web*. He watched it over and over. We had a VCR back then. We wore the tape out.

E.B. White, one of the greatest writers of the 20th century, wrote *Charlotte's Web*. He made Charlotte the spider a writer, too. She wrote messages in her web, but she talked some.

"After all, what's a life anyway?" Charlotte said to Wilbur the pig. "We're born, we live a little while, we die."

E.B. White, in *Charlotte's Web*, wrote, "Nobody, of the hundreds of people that had visited the Fair, knew that a gray spider had played the most important part of all. No one was with her when she died."

I Would Love to Write a Book Like a Stephen King Book

Chapter 5

I like Stephen King. I've seen all the movies about alien clowns and possessed dogs and cars and corn-children. I love his book *On Writing*, which is brilliant because it's about real life, writing and family and struggling with money and being hit by a van and facing mortality and getting depressed and trying to go on writing while his body was broken, and trying to believe in the world despite all that.

"We all make up horrors to help us deal with the real ones," Stephen King says.

"One word at a time," Stephen King says when people ask him how to write.

When faced with a blank page, I try to remember that.

When faced with a blank page, I think of my father, all the words he and I never spoke, or the words we spoke and how they meant other things we couldn't say.

I hate to think about horror, the reality. The other things my father showed me.

Stephen King, I love you.

You know the world is a nightmare, but you make it magic, too.

Still, *Carrie* breaks my heart.

Did she have to die in the end?

Yes, probably so.

Boring, Sidney

Chapter 6

The truth is, I'm at Panera because I'm hiding out. I haven't been writing at home because Locklin just graduated from high school and Phelan is on break and they're both already bored with summer. Phelan most of all.

"It's barely June," I say.

Phelan says, "It feels longer," and rolls her lovely green eyes.

"You couldn't wait for school to be out," I say.

"I'm bored," she says and gives the word two syllables. Bore-ed.

"Bored people are boring, Sidney," I say but my Zoomer daughter doesn't get the reference—Sid Vicious, Nancy Spungen, Johnny Rotten, the Sex Pistols, and so.

Oi oi oi oi oi.

The coffee refills here are limitless, so there's that, too.

When I lived in New York, I bought two turtles from a man who was selling turtles out of a bucket at the San Gennaro Festival, Little Italy, circa 1997.

Buying turtles off the street in New York is a terrible idea, but I was lonely and needed something to love, something tiny to ground me, maybe. The turtles were cute, the size of two fifty-cent pieces. At first, I let them chase each other in my crash-pad bathtub. I begged my crash-pad roommates to let them stay.

Flash-forward a few months—the turtles, whom I named Sid and Nancy, punk rock's nightmare Romeo and Juliet—were obviously illegal and, less obviously, carnivorous. They ate goldfish I'd have to buy from a pet store and sacrifice. The turtles didn't like the goldfish heads, so Sid and Nancy's tank would burble with severed fish heads, eyes bobbing this way and that. The fish heads smelled. The turtles smelled. The turtles' shells were slicked with salmonella and Nancy, in a moment of turtle- performance-art imitating life, started to attack Sid, a bit of his tail here, a chunk off one leg, then a whole leg.

Finally, I gave Sid and Nancy to a cop I knew in Queens whose kid loved turtles, legal or not.

"What can you do?" the cop said as he loaded Sid and Nancy's tank onto a dolly. "Kids are a pain in the ass. Relentless. Am I right?"

Those box turtles from my childhood—I knew not to move them, I knew what was wrong and why. I had no idea where Sid and Nancy fit, where their lives started, how they ended up in Queens, New York, but of course Queens wasn't their home.

We're talking continents away, probably. First a bucket. Then a bathtub. A fish tank. Store-bought goldfish as a sacrifice.

Nothing felt right.

"Don't you have any errands we can run?" my bored daughter, whom I don't consider a pain in the ass but who is, without doubt, relentless, says.

Which is how we ended up here. A mall Panera is a good compromise. I can hole up and write and Phelan can drop two hours in Hot Topic trying to decide between a Chakra bracelet and a *Beauty and the Beast* bracelet and a bracelet with miniature Ouija boards dangling from it like tiny brown teeth.

Phe texts me multiple pictures of bracelets, with a note that says, "I hate decisions!!!"

I text back and say she should go with the Chakras because they're pretty and Disney is always killing off mothers in its movies, and Ouija boards can be bad omens, despite the one I won at a bingo at St. Regis Church years ago, thinking it would provide enlightenment via the wisdom of the dead.

The Catholic Church, cool with gambling and exorcisms and indulgences, is usually against casual communing with dead people, but all the prizes at the bingo were donated, and we paid good money to play, and luck is luck. So I took the Ouija board home and showed my mother and thought maybe she'd be happy her daughter was a winner with a prize to show.

My mother burned the Ouija board in our fireplace. The smoke was probably toxic.

"Do you want to let the Devil into our house?" my mother said. "You idiot."

This was my mother's translation of Catholic Catechism, which says "Consulting horoscopes, astrology, palm reading, interpretation of omens, the phenomena of clairvoyance, and recourse to mediums all conceal a desire for power over time, history, and, in the last analysis, other human beings, and must be rejected."

Whatever. My mother ignored what she wanted to ignore.

A *Success Dream Book*, fine. "Dear Abby" columns and the daily horoscope? Sure.

A Ouija board in her house? No way.

"Father Mike was in charge of the bingo," I told my mother.

"Father Mike cares too much about his hair," my mother said.

Father Mike was suspicious because he was too handsome and not in a creepy way. Everyone from church ladies to elementary school kids crushed on him. He looked like George Harrison and played guitar and wore sandals and held open confessions, which were more like therapy sessions, one-on-one, face-to-face in a room, instead of the more traditional confessions at St. Regis, in that repurposed janitor's closet, with its creaky, red-padded kneeler, a yellowed honeycomb screen, the moth-balled air the only thing separating sinners from our other priest, Father Ackerman.

Father Ackerman did not approve of bingo.

Father Ackerman did not okay Ouija boards.

Father Ackerman did not smile or play guitar.

Father Ackerman did not easily offer indulgences.

Father Ackerman hated winners.

Father Ackerman hated everyone.

I hated Father Ackerman, Jesus have mercy.

Father Ackerman was ancient and hairy-eared and mean and completely un-crushable. Father Ackerman's hands, chapped and pale, looked like he washed them too many times, like Lady MacBeth, *out, damned spot*, and no one would want to see Father Ackerman's feet in sandals, dear God, not ever.

Father Ackerman's earlobes were rubber oysters.

Father Ackerman damned me and many of my friends too many times to count.

"Hopeless, hopeless," Father Ackerman would say, and prescribe 50 Hail Marys and 100 Our Fathers to wash us, not just our sins, away.

Helpless, helpless, Father Mike played on his guitar, channeling Neil Young.

I wanted the *Ouija* board to tell me I was neither hopeless nor helpless. I wanted the *Ouija* board to tell me I'd be a famous writer and I'd see Paris and maybe even Vienna, which Billy Joel sang about in the 1900s, *slow down, you crazy child.*

I wanted the Ouija board to tell me who I'd love and how long I'd live and so on.

It's important for a writer and a human to know how much time they have on this earth.

Which clock runs time in the afterlife?

Seriously. I'd like to know.

Maybe the Ouija would have told me what I know now.

Yes, Paris.

Yes, Vienna.

Yes, Madrid and Barcelona and Rome and New York.

Yes, Lorain, Ohio, and Atlanta, Georgia, and Ocean City, Maryland, and Memphis, Tennessee, and Greece and Paris and Madrid and Rome.

And home. Home.

Always that.

Neither helpless nor hopeless.

I'm 55 years old.

Your One Phone Call

Chapter 7

I am eating a Greek salad at Panera when my phone rings. I don't usually pick up, but it's been a week since my biopsy and I'm still sore and my right boob is bruised black and yellow, and I've been waiting days that have stretched on like 600 miles of bad road.

My boob looks like Gorbachev's forehead.

My boob looks like an ink blot.

"Who's Gorbachev?" my daughter, my Gen-Z-er, asks.

I say, "He tore down the Berlin Wall. Sort of."

There are bits of The Berlin Wall on display in Ocean City, Maryland, in Ripley's Believe It or Not! I have pictures of my daughter there, in front of the graffitied bits, written in English: "Don't Go with the Flow" and "Move with the Groove."

Rainbows.

Rainbows.

In whatever language, rainbows mean hope.

\ \ |

Gorbachev's forehead birthmark used to be called a port-wine stain. Many people had these when I was growing up, though I never see them now. Doctors, genetics, evolution, who knows.

In Gorbachev's forehead, I see a map of a small country that looks like it's melting. Crying, maybe.

"I believe in the cosmos," Gorbachev said when asked about his religious beliefs. "All of us are linked to the cosmos."

Rorschach, the father of ink blots, died at 37, precisely 18 years younger than I am now.

It's funny the things I think about lately. It's funny the kind of math I do when I usually shudder away all things math.

Did you know Rorschach looked like Brad Pitt?

Brad Pitt and Rorschach looked like Father Mike. They had amazing hair.

Do you remember Brad Pitt was once married to Gwyneth Paltrow?

Gwyneth Paltrow has a lot of ideas about hair and salads, self-care, and conscious uncoupling. Her company, Goop, sells a $3,490 solid gold dildo called Olga and a candle scented like Gwyneth's vagina. Gwyneth Paltrow's vagina candle, with hints of bergamot, costs $75, though it's often sold out and on back order.

Years ago, when I lived in New York, I saw Brad Pitt on the street scooping poop from a snippy little dog I think was Gwyneth's pup.

What the hell was wrong with you back then, Brad Pitt?

All ten of Rorschach's images look like vaginas and ovaries and pelvises. A few of them look like bunnies fighting. Another one looks like the Grecian urn—beauty is truth, truth beauty.

Brad Pitt played the Greek hero Achilles in the movie *Troy.*

On camera, Brad Pitt looks immortal, lit through with gold.

On the street in New York, Brad Pitt looked ordinary, another New Yorker scooping poop. Cute, kind, human, connected to us all through the cosmos.

My phone rings three times before I pick up.

Truth, beauty.

Beauty, truth.

Those Greek figures chasing each other around that vase, stalling for eternity.

I love the word "stalling." It's tiny, but clever, the way the vowels and consonants melt and stick like peanut butter in your mouth.

Stalling. Stalling.

Try it.

The word does what it says.

Isn't language magic?

See what I mean?

My phone's ringtone is the sound of typewriter keys.

A while back, at *The London Times*, editors pumped the sound of typewriters into the newsroom, a subliminal thing. The sound of typewriters, even for people who grew up without them, gets writers excited. The words come faster. The pages fill up. Good for deadlines. Good for profits. Writers pumped up on adrenaline move stories forward.

"This is," I finally say to the voice on the phone who asks to speak with me.

I spear an olive into my mouth.

My boob is a storm cloud.

My boob hurts so much.

Up until this phone call, I've been making jokes about my ink-blot boob. These jokes make people other than Newman uncomfortable.

Newman's dubbed my 3D-biopsied breast Frankenboob.

"Pitchforks! Fire bad!" he says and waves his arms.

I can't stop cracking Rorschach jokes.

"Tell me what you see," I say, and push my boob close to his face.

"My mother never breastfed me?" Newman says.

"I've heard that," I say.

"At least they didn't stab you in the ass," Newman says, and grabs my ass hard enough to bruise that too.

My ass is not the same as it was when we got married at a discount wedding chapel in Vegas. I never appreciated my ass back then, or that I could get away with wearing a white bikini at the pool during our honeymoon at Circus, Circus. It's been a few years since I've donned a bathing suit or asked for the lights on during sex, but my husband makes me feel beautiful.

Under Mikhail Gorbachev, the former Soviet Union practiced a policy called *glasnost*, a lovely word, which means openness and transparency. Truth.

Truth: I am grateful for my life.

I expect this new call from the oncology nurse to tell me everything is fine, it was just a scare, and I should expect another 20 years of love and ass-grabbing and jokes about fire and angry villagers.

"Can you speak up please?" I say.

The nurse's voice sounds muffled, like someone is holding a pillow between us to smother our words.

"Can you speak up, please?" I say again. I want to say, "Oh come on." I want to say, "We've been through this before," though I have no idea if this oncology nurse is the same oncology nurse I talked to last time around. So many doctors. So many nurses already.

I spear another olive and think how much I love olives and nurses. I'm thinking of a nurse who is not the nurse on the phone. I am thinking of a nurse with beautiful tattoos, the names of her children, some flowering vines.

During one of my cancer screenings, this nurse I'm thinking of ran tests on me and, somehow, we started talking about shaving our pussies.

"I knew this stripper once," the nurse said. "She told me her trick: a little toner and antibiotic cream, and *boom*, no more bumps."

-\\

I was at a strip club once in New Orleans. It was called "Big Daddy's."

Animatronic legs high-kicked over Big Daddy's entrance. The legs wore thigh-highs and red high heels. The bouncer who perched on a stool beneath the legs was a large woman with a buzz cut and black gauges the size of quarters in her ears. I loved and feared her from the start.

Inside, a beer was $12. The wallpaper was worn red velvet and everything smelled a little dank, moldy, wet cigarette butts on the beach after high tide.

Newman and I sat next to the stage while a stripper swizzled around a pole. The stripper had tattoos of flames all around her pussy. The stripper wore shoes I could never stand in, let alone dance or swirl a pole in. She had a cesarean scar, like my cesarean scar, pink, jagged, Frankenstein stitchery peeping out from all the flames.

"That looks like it hurt," my husband said, friendly, making small talk. He meant the tattoo, which stretched from the stripper's pussy to her ass. It was impressive, really. Intricate. Art. All vibrant reds and oranges and yellows.

I can't imagine how long it took. I assume the procedure was clinical—the stripper lying on an exam table, legs in stirrups, the tattoo artist with a headlamp on, the kind gynecologists and dentists and cartoon coalminers wear.

The stripper, obviously a mother, probably sweet off stage or at least someone who might be a friend, said, "Why? You want to touch it?" Her voice was a razor, mean, and touching at strip clubs, even I knew, is always off-limits.

She said it like she'd love to call in the bouncer, who was built like a pork chop, who knew karate or jiu-jitsu probably, who knew how to make people not touch each other, ever, no matter why, no matter how lonely or curious or lost.

I drank my $12 beer. It was skunked. The mandatory second beer was skunked too.

The strip club visit was supposed to be fun and sexy.

It wasn't.

When my sweet nurse said *boom* she did that karate chop thing professional wrestlers do—hands to crotch—*suck it, delete.*

"That's life-changing," I said.

The nurse said, "I know!" and chopped again.

We laughed and chatted and pulled our pants down to compare C-section scars and razor burns. We whined about bathing suits and what the hell, why should we care at our age? Lucky to be alive, lucky to get to the beach now and then.

That last part is from a line from Gerald Stern's great poem, "Lucky Life." Some poems live inside me, strands of DNA I can point to and name.

I want to tell the oncology nurse on the phone about my friend, the nurse with beautiful tattoos and no razor burn. I want to talk about my love of nurses in general because the nurse on the phone sounds so awkward, and I want her to be okay because I'm pretty sure I am okay, no need for this ongoing strangeness between us. I want to tell her my mother was a nurse, and that people called my mother Sarge because she wouldn't take any nonsense. I want to tell her Sarge was kind too, and how when I was a child in the hospital, my mother—Sarge the nurse—Slept on a cot next to my bed and worked double shifts so she could be with me.

Such is the love of a mother who is also a nurse.

"I'm sorry," the oncology nurse on the phone says, and I'm confused. I think I ask her name and maybe she tells me, but I forget it right away even though I try so hard not to do that.

Names connect us to each other. Names remind us that we're human. Knowing someone's name changes things. It's harder to be cruel. It's harder to lie.

When I sense awkwardness, when I feel other people's discomfort, I fill up the space between us with words. I talk. I keep talking.

You may have noticed this.

Indulgence.

Thank you for your patience, all these typewriters clacking in my mind.

The nurse on the phone whose name I don't know says sorry again, more pillowed things.

I stop talking and stop eating and look at my salad, all these extra olives.

Panera usually skimps on olives, so these olives are their own miracle.

A love or hate of olives is, scientists say, genetic. So is a love or hate of cilantro. Some people think cilantro tastes like lime. Other people think it tastes like soap.

I love olives. I love cilantro.

Nature over nurture, sometimes even on our tongues.

I love my mother, the mother who raised me. She loved olives, too. What my birth mother loves, I have no idea. Nature over nurture feels like a lie, a betrayal, at least.

After my daughter was born, I found my birth mother through Catholic Charities. I wanted a family medical history, "for my children," I said.

History of cancer? History of heart disease? History of mental illness?

My birth mother, whose name I know, refused. Instead, she wished me dead.

My birth mother has never called me by any name—neither the name she gave me nor the one my parents gave me. By keeping me nameless, she allows herself a necessary distance. Professional. Cool. She can protect her own heart. I understand. By keeping me nameless, my birth mother allows herself the space to be cruel. That part I understand less.

As I write this, my birth mother is still alive and my mother is not.

If I had to choose, I'd choose nurture over nature every time.

In a booth across from me, a mother feeds her tiny daughter something that looks like pudding. The girl, strapped into a highchair, doesn't like being locked down, so she bobs and weaves and the sprig of blonde hair ponytailed on top of her head burbles like a fountain, something to wish on.

In Rome I threw coins into a fountain. I've thrown coins into fountains in Paris, in Belgium, into a sad koi pond in Monroeville Mall. The fish in the koi pond died, I think, partly from all the coins and empty Orange Julius cups and cigarette butts people threw in there.

Poor sweet fish. All that filthy water. All those wishes.

Monroeville Mall, home country of *Dawn of the Dead,* which was filmed there. Monroeville, Pennsylvania, the birthplace of zombies.

"Help me," the little girl says, and her voice pops like bubble wrap.

Her mother says, "Shush now, you're fine," and spoons more pudding.

The nurse who is nameless tries twice to pronounce my last name.

"Close enough, no worries," I say.

I say, "It rhymes with tequila, but without the worm."

Funny. Funny. Always that.

"Everything's a joke to you," my father used to say to me. "Jackass."

The nurse on the phone doesn't laugh.

"Help," the little girl dodging the spoon says.

"Shush now, you're fine," her mother says.

"I'm sorry," the nurse says. Again. Again.

-\\

In Spain, there's a version of Panera called Pan Pan. Meat and cheese and bread. Everything a person needs to go on living.

My first time in Spain, and my second time, and my third time, I lived at Pan Pan. I knew what to order. *Carne. Queso. Pan.* I knew the order of things.

The little girl in her highchair sounds far away, her cries muffled by pudding.

The nurse says again, "I'm sorry."

The nurse says, "There's a malignancy."

I somehow ignore her.

At Pan Pan, the bread was pillowy, a cloud. *La nube.* Bread and cheese. Staples. All a person needs in this life.

The nurse says, "I am very sorry."

I think when people talk about leaving their bodies, near-death experiences, this is how it might feel, the untethering of that.

La nube. Lo siento. The cloud. I'm sorry.

One phone call like this.

"Shush now," the little girl's mother says. "You're scaring people."

"Stop scaring people," the doctor who wrote to me said.

I miss my mother.

I miss my mother.

The nurse does not say cancer. She says, "There is a malignancy."

When I was a flight attendant, in my other life, we were trained to call storms "weather" and turbulence "rough air," and a crash "a hard landing." A bomb threat was "an incident" and a hijacking was "a trip." A drink was "a beverage," no matter how weak or strong.

Never drink coffee or hot tea on an airplane. The water used for coffee and tea comes from the same source as the water used in the toilets. Planes are limited. The ice is suspect too.

Maybe everything on a plane, in the air, on the ground, causes cancer.

And yet every profession has a language meant to keep people calm. Every profession has its own language of kindness to protect people from panic and pain, to keep people believing we are tethered to this world.

In what world does the word "malignancy" sound better than cancer?

Ours, maybe.

More syllables at least.

"Do you want to touch it?" the stripper in New Orleans asked my husband. She spread her pussy like a map, then she pulled back, stomped a heel off the ledge of the stage, and knocked my second $12 Heineken to the ground.

Gwyneth Paltrow was on my flight once.

Gwyneth fake-gagged and threatened everyone and required oxygen because she thought her first-class vegetarian meal may have nestled against her seatmate's prime rib.

Malignant! Malignancy!

Gwyneth, who friends call Gwynnie, fanned her face like she was on fire. She stuck out her pretty pink tongue so I could check it for poison.

Gwyneth's lovely baby-butt complexion splotched over as her anger flared. Her seatmate, his meat bleeding a bit, looked mortified.

Their meals never touched, I swear.

Whatever, Gwyneth Paltrow, you beautiful, rich creep.

May you live forever even so.

On the phone, the nurse's voice has the tentativeness of someone who's uncomfortable speaking, though she, like me, fills the air between us with a lot of words.

She says, "I don't think we've met before."

She says, "Not that we're meeting, actually."

She says, "I'm sure we will meet at some point, but I didn't want you to wait. Waiting's the worst, right? And the doctor is on vacation. The Bahamas, actually. Or maybe it's Aruba. I get confused."

I've been to Aruba.

I've been to the Bahamas.

In Nassau, I ate conch fritters and rented a rusty Volkswagen, a stick shift, and tried to drive it on the wrong/right side of the road without stalling, but I gave up and got a bicycle instead. The bike wobbled a lot. The brakes worked only sometimes. Later, I rented a jet ski and took it out, even though I'm a terrible swimmer and terrified of sharks. But the jet ski was cheap and came with a life jacket.

I wish everything in this world came with a life jacket.

The water was blue and clear and seemed safe, as if I could see straight to the bottom of the ocean, as if I could see danger coming and get out of the way.

The ocean looked shallow as a bathtub.

The ocean looked endless as the universe.

I didn't think about death then, not even with my fear of sharks and drowning.

How long ago was that?

I try to do the math.

Over 20 years.

"We're here for you," the nurse on the phone says.

Limited. The choices at Big Daddy's. Gwyneth Paltrow's palate. The choices of words we have for moments like this.

The nurse says, "If you need us or have questions."

The little girl in her highchair says, "No," and starts to cry harder.

My tits hurt and I don't know if it's the nurse's words that make it so or if it's real.

I want to ask but I don't know how.

What should I feel? What shouldn't I feel?

How does anyone know if they're dying when we all are, all the time, really, even so?

"Did it hurt?" my husband asked the stripper at Big Daddy's.

All those flames. All those needles.

I had my own questions for the stripper, too, but I kept quiet.

Tattoos before the C-section or after?

How many children?

What are their names?

What's your name?

Can we be friends?

I had my first C-section after 21 hours of labor with my son. My daughter's birth was scheduled, and she came out through the same scar, easy-peasy.

Imagine coming into the world through all those tattooed flames.

There's a song by one of my favorites, Ike Reilly. "Born on Fire." It's so heartbreaking and good. Give it a listen if you can. It's a story, like all of Ike's songs are stories, but this one is about a father who can't answer his son's questions about faith and love and where we go when we die.

I'd love to know the stripper's story. I'd love to know everyone's story. There's so little we can do for one another. I write a lot about people I love who've died. It's a way to keep them alive. It feels less lonely, having them here on the page.

"Writers aren't people exactly," F. Scott Fitzgerald said. "They're a whole lot of people trying so hard to be one person."

That too.

In the Womancare Waiting Room, I Consider Flamingos

Chapter 8

The pink robes at Womancare smell like bleach. I wonder how many times they've been washed and reused. I wonder how many women have worn the robe I am wearing, how many of them were fine, how many were not fine, where they are now, if they have healed, if they are still here at all.

My mother wore a robe like this, many times.

My mother loved the color pink. Her favorite lipstick was from Sephora, a color called Pink Flamingo, the lipstick she wanted to wear in her casket because it would clash with her red suit and light her up like a love letter about to be buried.

"It really brightens up my face," she'd always say and purse her Flamingo'd lips into a kiss in the mirror.

My beautiful mother.

My sad lonely funny mother.

When she died, I found tubes of Pink Flamingo in her dresser drawer. I found tissues she used to blot.

"Make sure they use my lipstick," my mother said when she was planning her own funeral. "Not some of that Frankenstein crap."

All these tissues in my mother's dresser looked like shrouds, the imprint of my mother's kiss on them, a holy thing.

I should have kept them.

I wish I had.

In 1985, a 15-year-old boy was arrested for throwing rocks at African Great flamingos in the Pittsburgh Zoo. One of the rocks hit a flamingo and severed its leg.

The bird died, euthanized.

"It was pretty," the boy said. "I was just trying to make it fly."

It's strange the things that happen while you're waiting.

It's strange the things fear makes you think about.

Pink breast-cancer ribbons look like flamingos.

Breast cancer ribbons pinned on breasts look like pink markers on graves.

In the waiting room at Womancare, most of us avoid conversation and eye contact. Most of us flip through our phones. A few of us, when our phones lose power, resort to the outdated magazines that fleck the sturdy end tables—*People, Good Housekeeping, Parenting.*

Back in the waiting rooms of my childhood, *Highlights* Magazine had a feature, "Goofus and Gallant." The comic featured Goofus, a jerk, and Gallant, a kind boy who believed in righteousness above all things. The purpose of the comic was to teach children kindness. Good/bad. Right/wrong.

"Be kind babies," Kurt Vonnegut said.

My phone is dead.

A soap opera is on one overhead TV, a talk show on the other.

The talk show is hosted by Dr. Oz, an episode about the dangers of buying underwear in department stores. People, it seems, are buying panties and bras and wearing them before washing them first. Dr. Oz and his team of True Crime experts are investigating store-return policies. Far too many stores, Dr. Oz has discovered, restock used underwear and unsuspecting customers are buying them.

"Isn't that illegal?" Dr. Oz, his famous eyebrows in a cartoon-villain arch, his voice a gasp, asks his research staffers, who say, "Absolutely, Dr. Oz."

Dr. Oz's staffers purchase 11 pairs of underwear from top chain stores and send them out to a lab for testing. All but one test positive for coliform bacteria. Half the samples also contain trace amounts of yeast. All but two samples are soiled with mold. No one has gotten sick from wearing store-bought, unwashed panties, but still.

The terror! The fear!

We live in an era of pre-emptive strikes.

I watch Dr. Oz, that jackass, hold up a fistful of poison panties in this pink-robed waiting room and imagine everything in the world is out to kill us all.

"I'll save you!" Gallant from *Highlights* would say.

But no one can save anyone, I think.

Alex Trebek from *Jeopardy* had cancer.

I try to think of answers in the form of questions.

In the waiting room, an older woman talks loudly to no one. The woman wears shiny silver sandals. Our shoes, I start to realize, are one of the things that tell us apart.

The other thing is hair, its presence or absence. This woman's hair is stubbled from chemo or radiation, maybe both. Another woman in the room is completely bald.

My father. His hair. How, if he fell asleep, he'd furiously reach around until he found his knit cap, the way people with bad eyesight grapple for their glasses before they open their eyes.

My father felt shame. I feel shame. I feel shame for worrying about my hair. I feel shame for worrying about chemo and radiation, even though the doctor told me not to worry about any of that yet. I feel shame for my own vanity, how much I fear chemo, the effects of that, the privilege of fearing the effects of that.

My hair is past my shoulders. I have been letting it grow and grow and I keep it dyed blonde, even though the hair at my temples is almost pure white.

Here, in this place, my hair seems wrong, obnoxious.

More Goofus than Gallant.

I should have tied my hair back. I should have cut it to be decent.

The color feels fake and loud and shallow, yellow as a hazard sign, yellow as yield, yellow as the lemons bobbing in the water cooler, dead jaundiced fish.

Later, after all the surgeries that will save my life, I will let my hair grow and keep growing.

I will tell people I'm letting it grow before the doctors take it from me.

I will tell people I'm letting it grow to see how long it will get.

I don't want my children to have to see me bald.

I will say, "With cancer, you never know how long you have."

I will say this as a joke.

I will laugh but it and my hair will make people uncomfortable. It will make me uncomfortable too, but I will be out of touch with the part of myself that can say why.

Today, the woman who talks to herself is worried about parking, her meter expiring, how long she has been waiting. I want to offer to check her meter, to put some money in, but something about the waiting room, about the way none of us looks at one another, like we are afraid whatever we are waiting on is contagious—contagious, when we have already caught our own diseases, when we are *diseased*, what a word—keeps me quiet.

"I swear," the woman is saying, "if I get a bullshit ticket on top of all this there will be hell to pay."

The waiting room smells like lilies and roses.

Funeral flowers, I think. Lovely even so.

There is a snack basket here, always a bad sign, a sign that things in this place are serious enough to require snacks.

This snack basket is filled with Smart Popcorn and granola bars. Everything healthy.

I touch my hair despite myself. I pull strands to see if they hold. I examine the damage, split ends. I put a strand in my mouth the way I did as a nervous child.

"Stop that," my mother would say.

I smooth the wet strand back down.

Still here.

I Got You, Babe

Chapter 9:

Before my mother died of breast cancer, she and I went through boxes of old photos to display at her funeral: my mother as a young girl on a horse at Kennywood Park, my mother in her wedding dress pelting my father with cake, my mother in a green bikini at Miami's South Beach.

"I can't believe that was my body," my mother said about the bikini.

I am adopted, yes.

I am my mother's daughter.

There is a picture somewhere of me in a bikini, Ocean City, Maryland, circa 2002. I barely recognize myself.

"The doctor gave you a bikini cut," the nurses said after my first C-section, "so you'll still look sexy on the beach."

My mother and I in bikinis, not knowing we'd ever grow old.

"Make sure you put that one up," my mother said about her bikini picture. "It will make everyone crazy."

My mother liked to think of her death as a way to stick it to people who annoyed her in this life. Her requests: to be buried in a bright red suit, her lips tinted in her favorite shade of pink lipstick, the colors of a Valentine, sticky candy hearts.

"And none of that mortuary makeup," my mother said. "I don't want to look dead for Christ's sake."

My mother's request: the remembrance board should include pictures both her sisters and the priests would think inappropriate.

The bikini picture, for example.

My mother's boobs were extraordinary.

It is impossible not to see them and go on seeing them.

She was so beautiful.

When my mother was young, her older sisters would make her hide in the attic when their boyfriends visited. The sisters were terrified their boyfriends would fall in love with my mother. She was that beautiful and curvy and fun and sweet.

I look nothing like my mother, adoption and so. I wish I did. But we're the same in spirit nonetheless, the same in our desire to be beautiful and seen, or rebellious and dangerous enough for people to want to hide us away.

"That will show them," my mother said about the photos she picked for her own funeral. I loved that.

My mother, funny, beautiful, and a little spiteful to the end.

In the photos, she looks like Sophia Loren.

Sophia Loren is still alive, one of the last surviving stars of the Golden Age of Hollywood.

In 2021, Netflix released a documentary called *What Would Sophia Loren Do?* It's the story of Nancy Kulik, a mother and grandmother who finds strength and joy through the work of her idol, Sophia Loren.

"I don't understand people who hide from their past," Sophia Loren said about the past and the pain it brings. "Everything you live through helps to make you the person you are now."

My mother and I went through the photos at the request of the funeral director, who prided himself on his remembrance boards, which were huge and bedazzled, the deceased's name in glitter and fairy lights.

The bulletin boards, the funeral director said, were a highlight of the remembrance ceremony, which is what he called the visiting hours before a burial.

"People like to remember the good times. A celebration of life even in death," the funeral director said, raising his eyes to the ceiling, beseeching.

This is something I'm sure he rehearsed and said many times.

The funeral director was famous among middle-schoolers. He'd volunteer at Fun Day, an event that featured inflatable bouncy houses and a huge Velcro wall. The funeral director always volunteered for The Velcro wall. He'd dress up in a Velcro suit, fling himself off a trampoline and get stuck on the wall, where he'd cling a bit until cute girls would pry him down. For a grown man to fling himself at a Velcro wall is a celebration of life in a way. Defy gravity. Defy death. And so it goes.

My mother believed in the funeral director's family and made it clear in her directives that she wanted his family to handle her body.

"We'll take care of her like she was our own," the funeral director said, and lifted his eyes again toward the Velcro heaven that paid him.

My mother's remembrance ceremony featured tins of Danish cookies and carafes of bad coffee and lukewarm tea. The remembrance ceremony was held in the lobby of our town's funeral home. The funeral home had relocated to a former auto repair shop. It still smelled like tires and gasoline, burnt metal and an oil change. Things that could be fixed: a car engine, brake pads, anything not human.

"Would you like to say a few words?" the funeral director asked me, and I couldn't speak.

Grief.

Just the word catches in your throat. In my throat. The linguistic beauty and horror of that.

My husband spoke for my mother. He talked about the bathing suit she bought late in life, an age-appropriate one-piece, and how she was embarrassed to be seen in it but how much she loved the water and the sun, and how neighbors invited her to swim in their above-ground pool and how she loved her neighbors and how she couldn't say no to anyone she loved.

My mother loved my husband so much.

Lucky life, my husband said, again quoting as I go on quoting Gerald Stern, our beloved Pittsburgh homeboy, who knew something about what it meant to go on living even so.

The poet Kate Daniels wrote that it's best to think of Gerald Stern as "post-nuclear. A multicultural Whitman for the millennium. Our one and truly global poet."

Born in 1925, Gerald Stern is still with us as I write this. Gerald Stern was my teacher back in the 1900s, early 1990s to be precise. We were at a writers' conference in Vermont, that heaven for writers, all those green mountains and arugula and sheep, and Gerry's car was on the fritz. So, I drove the great poet to the repair shop where his car was getting repaired.

Gerald Stern popped a tape into the tape deck in my car. This was the 1900s and so tape decks and cassettes were a thing. These will have a resurgence with my daughter and all Zoomers around now because of the static in the sound, the way it seems more authentic, human, true. Or at least cool.

I saw a t-shirt the other day. It said, "Never Forget," and I thought of 9/11, the towers falling, but no. The shirt had three images: a boombox, a vinyl record, and a cassette tape. I love that, I think.

Gerry Stern's cassette tape was a recording of a Jewish cantor singing a song about fallen people. The great poet rolled down the window of my old car—rolling windows down was also a thing in the 1900s, hand cranks, it took a minute—and leaned out.

He sang along and waved his arms as I drove.

The music of the cantor was neither beautiful nor not beautiful.

Gerald Stern's singing voice was terrible and beautiful.

A great poet waving his arms out of my rusted, rattling car into the green Vermont valleys and mountains felt, still feels, like magic. A blessing, maybe.

"May their memory be a blessing," my Jewish friends say when people die.

What a beautiful thing to say when words fail.

All these accidental moments, these bits of unexpected sweetness, that make up a life.

I was in a car accident back in the 1900s. It wasn't a bad accident, though it could have been. The paramedics and a cop and a tow truck driver all called me lucky, and I was. But here's the thing: as my car was spinning out, as I headed toward a concrete beam, as I waited for the impact that somehow never came, the radio kept playing.

Cher.

"If I Could Turn Back Time."

Dear God. What a terrible song.

As my car spun, I kept thinking the radio should have the decency to shut itself off. After my car stopped and I realized I was somehow fine, Cher kept on singing.

Cher never learned to sing. What an actress. What a personality. What a beautiful heart. What a great tattooed ass.

When confronting one's own mortality there shouldn't be a soundtrack. Or, if there is a soundtrack, it shouldn't be Cher, who was married to Sonny Bono, who used to wear a furry vest and love beads before he became a congressman.

Sonny Bono died when he crashed into a tree while skiing at Lake Tahoe.

I imagine the soundtrack of his death was not "I Got You Babe."

It was ice and snow and wind.

When Cher dies, the soundtrack will be Cher.

Back in Panera, the nurse on the phone says, "I want you to know we're here for you. The doctor will be back next week to go over everything and talk about the next steps."

It takes her so long to get to the biopsy results that her voice, tired maybe, sounds robotic, legs kicking over the entrance to "Big Daddy's."

It's clear the nurse is reading from a computer chart.

She says, "You're lucky. If you have to have one, this is the one to have."

Her voice sounds like a child trying to wink.

How many of these calls does she have to make in one day? What does her real voice, the one she uses at home, sound like?

Winking is hard. It takes practice.

I remember trying to teach my son, then my daughter to wink. It's not a natural thing. Also, how to whistle. And snap fingers. Such essential human things are not simple at all.

I sort the nurse's words the way I'd sort avocados at the grocery, looking for the good ones, the ones with just enough give to hold a fingerprint.

There aren't any good ones.

Lucky, maybe.

I wonder how many of these calls the nurse makes in a week, a month, a year.

I wonder where all the people she calls are when they pick up their phones, everything ordinary then not.

They Write Your Name on a Grain of Rice

Chapter 10

"How are you holding up?" the doctor asks, something no one wants to hear a doctor ask.

I focus on the doctor's clogs. Expensive.

Her hair. Expensive.

Her eyeglasses. Expensive, German.

When I was a flight attendant, I could always tell German passengers by their serious eyeglasses and the assiduous way they followed the safety demo. My birth mother is Irish. My birth father was German. I love the Pogues. I have several pairs of serious eyeglasses. I have several serious perspectives, all of them evolving. Conflict rages inside me.

The doctor shows me cross-sections of my breasts on her computer screen. The images look like something from the Weather Channel, a satellite tracking a monochrome storm.

"You see here," the doctor says, pointing out a line of tiny white spots, innocent as grains of rice. "And also here."

At New York City street fairs, there's always a booth claiming: *We write your name on a grain of rice.*

Why write someone's name so tiny it can't be seen without a magnifying glass?

Why write someone's name on a medium so fragile it's bound to dissolve or turn to dust?

Who perfects an art like that?

When the doctor shows me the cross-section of my breasts, the grains inside, the microscopic tears that beckon my death, I think: *Oh they're pretty.*

Rice writing began in ancient Anatolia, in Turkey.

Wearing a rice grain with your name on it brings good fortune.

Wearing a rice grain with your name on it heightens fertility.

Flat long-grain is best for longevity.

The next time I come across a rice-writing booth, I will have a grain etched with my name and dangle it on a silver chain.

I will pass this on, an heirloom for my children.

The doctor's unmanicured finger connects the grains on the screen, as if what she is showing me will take shape and make sense.

Why does a woman with so much money and style not get manicures? I was a flight attendant. When flight attendants start out, we're pretty poor, but the company still required manicures. Manicures meant you cared about passengers. Manicures meant you wouldn't offend people when you handed them a Coke.

I am not offended by the doctor's fingers. They are honest and sturdy. They trace a trusty line between the rice grains, a connect-the-dots puzzle, *Highlights*, Goofus and Gallant.

What's hidden in this picture? Look, an apple! Look, a puppy!

"And here," the doctor says.

Look, cancer.

I'd be sad whenever I opened a copy of *Highlights* and some other kid had already connected all the dots. Mystery ruined.

The dots on the doctor's computer look like the freckles on my left thigh.

The freckles lined up like the Big Dipper. I always thought this meant something special.

"When we brought you home from the orphanage, there wasn't a spot on you," the mother who raised and loved me said. "You were perfect then."

"That," my mother said of the constellation on my skin, "came later."

She sounded disappointed.

My mother changed my birth name from Amelia to Lori.

Lori would be easier to fit on a grain of rice.

Lori is the name of a kind of parakeet.

Once, at a county fair, I went into a room filled with red lories, bright fluttering hearts.

"Nothing but trouble," the room attendant said about the birds, then spit.

Red lories require toys to keep them occupied. They are temperamental, always looking for adventure.

In the netted room, one lory perched on my shoulder.

Another shit on my head.

"When they line up like that," the doctor says about my rice grains, "it's concerning."

When I was twelve, I changed my name from Lori to Willow, as in weeping. I cried a lot back then. My mother gave me a nickname—Cry Baby Duck. She bought me a book with that as a title. She read it aloud every night, hoping to break me.

It's the book my daughter calls child abuse. Who would ever do that to a child?" my daughter says any time the subject comes up, and looks like she might cry.

"Give the waterworks a rest," my mother used to say.

No one would call me Willow, not even my father, who loved me most of all.

At some point, I stopped crying.

I tried to be sensible.

When her breast cancer came, my mother took my hand and put it on the lump doctors told her not to worry about.

"Can you feel it?" my mother asked.

I had to resist the urge to pull my hand away.

I touched it with two fingers.

I still feel it now, such is the tangible memory of death in my mother's body, now in my body, which feels too young to die.

"I'm sure it's nothing," I said, and did not cry.

"You can see how they're aligned?" the doctor says.

The rice grains line up like soldiers, tiny plastic army men my children played with for years, battalions on windowsills, my pillow, battles raging everywhere.

"Are you crying?" my son and daughter who have never seen me

cry will ask later.
They will check my eyes for tears.

Proof of Life

Chapter 11

When I worked for the airlines, I flew with one former Dallas Cowboys cheerleader and one former Rockette and one former Hooters girl. When we worked together, I—with my graduate degree in poetry, the kick-line skills of an arthritic flamingo, no boobs worth mentioning, and the athletic prowess of a boulder—hobbled around like Quasimodo in the presence of glimmering Esmeraldas.

I'd warm my hideous ordinary self in the light of my other-worldly beautiful friends, consoled only by my ability to recite multiple poems by William Blake, which seemed its own kind of glimmer at first, then not.

What immortal hand or eye / Could frame thy fearful symmetry?

I'd smooth my unexceptional hair, rub my tongue over my front teeth to clear them of lipstick, and duck into the lav to check my nostrils for snot.

"Hunting bats in the cave," flight attendants call this nose-check because passengers are always at nose level and can see right up there, and who wants to offend anyone like that?

Often, I worked the trash cart—a job that, unofficially, went to flight attendants who were not astonishingly beautiful enough to hide in the cockpit when there was real work to do. Flight attendants like me, who handed out airplane meals and retrieved the residue thereof, were rarely featured in the company safety videos and TV commercials.

"She's a workhorse," European flight attendants would say about me and people like me.

I grew up in Pittsburgh, working class. I'm proud of my work ethic. I believe work made and goes on making me something resembling a decent human. I tried to think of *workhorse* as a compliment, but in New York City, where I lived and worked, those words, lulled off the tongues of lovely Europeans and rich New Yorkers, sounded wrong, insulting even.

Workhorse.

Work.

Horse.

"Your trash?" I'd say, over and over, pushing the trash cart around passengers' outstretched legs and arms, gathering cups and leaky diapers and the dregs of airplane chicken, thinking of David Sedaris, one of my writer-heroes, a million-miler on my airline, rock star of the skies, and how he translated that phrase in an essay once to "You're trash. You're trash. You're trash."

Some days, that slap-back is all I needed to go on living.

"You're trash," I'd say to anyone who was cruel to me, and to myself when I was sad.

I'd wheel my squeaky cart, my own redemption song, up and down the aisle until landing.

As for my Hooters friend, she made the Hooters Calendar years before she was hired by the airline. She'd been Miss February, my birth month. My friend pretended to be embarrassed of this, but she kept copies of the calendar with her and would show them off when asked.

Imagine being able to freeze yourself and your life on a calendar, a date, a year.

I was here.

And I was gorgeous.

Here's a calendar.

Look, here's my page.

The phrase *proof of life* is most often used during kidnappings.

Hold up a newspaper. Hold up a calendar. Show the time on a watch.

Show you're alive now, today, in this moment.

Later, who knows?

Dark, right?

I have always hated having my picture taken, but late in my life, I've been blessed with Irish friends, those masters of dark humor. My best friend from Galway, Sinead, told me once, when I cringed and ducked a camera shot, "You'll never be as young and beautiful as you are right this second." She said, "Smile now, before Death sees you frowning."

She said, "If Death sees you frowning, he'll think you're ready to go."

Bless my Irish sweet ones.

Bless you, my beautiful Miss February.

Your lovely smile and boobs frozen in time, defying Death, long before the dawn of Photoshop and filters.

Way back in the 1900s, Phelan my Zoomer would say.

Miss February.

May you forever reign.

Hooters forced all their waitresses to wear Sheer Energy Suntan support hose, tiny construction-cone-orange booty shorts, and water bras called Miracles.

The Hooters' logo was a creepy owl with bulging eyes that everyone thought was clever because the eyes doubled as the Os in Hooters and, also, boobs.

"Oh dear God no, just no," Phelan says, and rolls her big green eyes.

Most Hooters have closed, but there's still one in Ocean City, Maryland. I know because we go there as a family almost every summer—to Ocean City, not Hooters. I hope we make it there this summer or even the next summer, or the next, but my cancer, my breasts trying to kill me, surgeries, more surgeries—that comes later.

For now, I'm thinking of the beach: my son, Locklin, bronzed and muscled as an action figure, stretched out, serious as a math equation on a towel; Phelan, her blonde pigtails bouncing as she rushes the waves, daring them to body slam her; my husband, Newman, following Phelan, waving to me from waist-high water while I try not to worry he'll be eaten by a shark or Phelan will be eaten by a shark or they'll both be swept under by a riptide.

I am terrified of the ocean.

Every year, I pretend I'm not.

I am terrible at pretending.

To me, everyone I love who bobbles in the ocean looks like a chicken nugget, every dark-capped wave a fin and razor teeth.

I breathe in the salt air and coconut lotion and try not to ruin things.

I slurp Hurricanes and piña coladas.

I hide my imperfect body in a black one-piece bathing suit and swath that over with a lacy coverup. I glaze myself with self-tanner, probably toxic, and think of an old *Cathy* cartoon strip where Cathy decides tanned fat looks like muscle.

"I get it. The 1900s," Phelan says when I try to explain newspapers and cartoon strips.

To see the world in a grain of sand, William Blake said. *To hold infinity in the palm of your hands.*

"Okay," Phelan says when I recite Blake and other poets I love, though she stretches the word out like a horizon, then goes back to scrolling TikTok.

I wonder if William Blake ever dug his toes into the sand he immortalized.

I wonder if Emily Dickinson ever went to the beach.

If she did, I wonder what Emily thought of the lovely, ravenous, and terrifying seagulls.

Cotton candy wasn't invented until 1894, 11 years after Emily died, so that was out.

Suntan lotion didn't show up until 1944, and Emily was so pale.

Saltwater taffy was around in the late 1800s and one legend says it was invented when a storm caused ocean water to flood a candy shop and washed over candy-in-progress.

Emily would have loved that, I think.

I hate salt-water taffy but each year I buy some anyway, because it's magic, an ocean on your tongue.

Sometimes in Ocean City, you can see schools of dolphins leaping, out past the waves, the way William Blake saw angels leaping in his backyard, maybe, all beauty and magic.

Dolphins have been known to protect humans from shark attacks.

Shark attacks on humans are rare.

Fun fact: most shark attacks happen in waist-high water.

Fun fact: Ocean City, Maryland is the only coastal U.S. city to never have had an unprovoked shark attack.

Still, over the entrance to the Ripley's Believe It or Not! museum in Ocean City Maryland, there's a huge animatronic great white shark, its tail thrashing, its jaws opening and closing, always so hungry.

Inside Ripley's, there's a room devoted to shark attacks. There's a diving cage with bars crushed by a great white. There's another cage where tourists can go inside and get their pictures taken. Behind the diving cage is a huge shark, mouth wide open, all those teeth.

Every year, I take pictures with my children in that cage. We pose like we're about to be chewed and swallowed.

In the shark room at Ripley's, they pipe in the soundtrack from *Jaws.*

Later this year, two fishermen will catch and release not one, but two great white sharks off the coast of Ocean City. Both sharks will be about 10 feet long and around 500 pounds. People will be shocked, but experts like Chris Fischer of Ocearch have always known better. Ocean City is in the migratory path of great whites. Ocean City is pretty much a great white nursery.

"Everyone on the East Coast is swimming with white sharks all the time and they always have been," Fischer said in an interview with *USA Today.* "Nothing has changed. The difference is we just know now."

And yet no one's been killed by a great white shark in Ocean City, Maryland.

The logical magic of that.

Here's a thing about cancer.

Everyone at any given time has damaged cells in their body.

Cells with damaged DNA have the potential to go rogue. Damaged cells are supposed to die off. When they don't die off as they should, they can become cancerous. It's like staying at a party too long. Go home already.

Lots of things weigh in with cancer: genetic mutations, things you're exposed to in everyday life, stress, stress, more stress, etc.

No one knows why some damaged cells become cancerous and others don't.

Those damaged cells are swimming in everyone, always.

"The difference is," Chris Fischer said about the sharks we all swim with, "we know now."

Shark research is clearly ahead of cancer research.

"We're going to need a bigger boat," Chief Brody says in *Jaws.*

When I was very young, maybe around the same time my father gave me a lesson in drowning, he took me to see *Jaws.* I was already afraid of pools, but *Jaws* made me afraid of our bathtub, like a shark might swim up through the plumbing.

"That will teach you," my father said that time I thought he'd drown me.

I suppose my father's lessons in fear taught me something—to be careful, maybe. I suppose there are a million better ways to learn. I don't swim now unless you count back floats. I can float on my back in a shark-free pool for days.

My father could be cruel, but I know now, having kids of my own, that he was also terrified. My father could be cruel and violent because the world he knew was cruel and violent and maybe he was trying in his way to inoculate me.

I learned something else from my father: Don't let fear make you mean.

Don't let fear make you hurt the people you love.

I'm trying.

I am.

When Newman takes Phelan into the water, I put my hand on my son's chest. I turn away from the ocean and focus on all the kites flying above the beach.

There is a kite shop in Ocean City called The Kite Loft. The Kite Loft makes amazing kites. Dragons, jellyfish, sharks, Squeaky the Octopus, The Red Baron, giant pigs.

How clever is that?

Pigs in the sky!

A miracle, really.

Back in 2000, a woman was kicked off a US Airways flight because her 300-pound emotional-support pig began squealing and walking up and down the aisle. As support animals go, pigs are smart, even though they aren't exactly flight friendly.

Pigs are smarter than dogs, have excellent memories, and, when piglets are born, the mother assigns each piglet its own teat from which the piglet never strays.

I learned my fun pig facts from one of my fellow flight attendants, Marie, who had a pet pig named Janice that had become famous among flight crews. Marie carried a photo album filled with pictures of Janice dressed up like celebrities–Marilyn Monroe, Dolly Parton, Johnny Cash. Marie was good with a sewing machine and Janice seemed amenable.

"She is so smart," Marie would say, proud as any parent with a bumper-stickered mini-van. "You can see it in her eyes."

Janice's eyes were lovely pig eyes, long-lashed deep pools.

Marie lived alone with Janice. Janice would, if it came to that, eat Marie, pigs also being ravenous and capable of consuming a human body without much trouble.

This is often a plot point in horror novels and gangster movies.

It's an awful thought.

Poor Marie.

Poor Janice.

Poor everybody.

Love doesn't have to make you cruel. Fear and love are not the same.

I've learned that.

It may be the only thing I know for sure.

Raised Catholic, I am lapsed forever, but sometimes when my husband and daughter are having fun in the possibly-shark-filled waves, I pray anyway. I use the words in my head I was made to recite as a child. *Mercy. Mercy.*

I keep my hand on Locklin's chest if he'll let me.

Sometimes he'll swat me away.

At some point, to have your mother hold onto you becomes an embarrassment. To have your mother hold onto you makes you feel weak and vulnerable, though it's the other way around.

Locklin doesn't like the ocean either. As my first-born, I scared him the most, I think.

I made him watch *Jaws.*

I made him watch *Jaws 2* and *Jaws 3.*

I am more like my father than I'd hoped.

On the beach, I watch those seagulls dive-bomb for fries from Thrasher's. I hold my son's hand and I'm grateful when he lets me.

Maybe one day he'll remember my hand on his, holding him, grounding him to this earth.

For now I watch a giant pig kite dip and float and fly above the waves.

My family and I go to Ocean City because Newman loves Ocean City and the kids love Ocean City and it's what we can afford. Newman lived there when he was in his late teens and when we're there as a family we map his past. Almost nothing in Ocean City changes, and almost all of it is filled with raunchy jokes made to poke through the veneer. All the people who cancel people canceled Ocean City long ago for its T-shirt slogans alone.

Big Pecker's Saloon's T-shirt says, "If It Swells, Ride It."

Brass Balls' Saloon's T-shirt claims, "You Gotta Have Brass Balls to Drink Here." There's the generic "Ocean City—We Got Crabs," and Salty Dog Saloon's "Bite

Me (The Best 8 Inches Your Mouth Ever Tasted)."

And, of course, there's The Bearded Clam bar, where the slogan is, "No Muff Too Tough We Dive At Five."

It's dirty and lovely and, kind of, true.

All that said, Ocean City is the most family-friendly place I've been. It's the only place where, at the boardwalk games, the vendors cheat to make sure kids win big stuffed animals or the blow-up guitars of their dreams. It's the only place, New York City aside, where I hear at least six or more languages spoken at the hotel pool. Ocean City's crazy-quilt of humans–Brown, Black, white; immigrants and beach-locals; queer, straight and otherwise; working-class folks and people who can afford all-you-can-eat seafood all day every day—seem to get along fine.

Most summers, our family walks the boardwalk and we come back to our hotel laden with prizes. We buy T-shirts and beach hats and $5 hoodies because the air off the ocean is chilly even in August. We stop by the Haunted Hideaway, where Newman worked, and the kids and I ask him again to tell us stories about how he and his friends would smear makeup on their faces to look like ghouls. Sometimes one of them would get so drunk the others would prop him up in a chair like a corpse. Customers, Newman says, screamed at the drunk corpse's slightest twitch.

"People would poke him and think he was really dead," Newman says. "It was so dark in there Marines would run out pissing their pants."

I love my husband's stories. Sharks aside, I've grown to love Ocean City, too, though it would never have been my first or last pick of vacation spots.

When we were first married, I still had my airline flight benefits. I lived in New York and Pittsburgh and had been flying for years. I'd been pretty much everywhere. Paris. Rome. Barcelona, Madrid. Paris. Paris.

"We can fly anywhere we want for free!" I told Newman, and thought he'd be excited. At the airline where I worked, we even had T-shirts: "Marry Me. Fly Free." And people think The Bearded Clam shirts are offensive.

But flight benefits are amazing. The world opens up, especially for working-class people like me who, pre-airline, had been mostly nowhere.

When I think of my life and whether or not I'm ready to leave it, I think of how many lifetimes I've lived and I feel lucky, but greedy, too—wanting more, always more.

Newman said, "Ocean City?" and I said, "Paris?"

Newman said, "Ocean City?" and I said, "Madrid?"

Newman said, "OC?" and I said, "We can drive there," and he said "Okay."

Newman is a practical, grounded person. He's never had money. He always lived like a man without money, a man without money who wants to write books.

His dreams were to hold still and write, not travel. I misunderstood that for years.

I have never been a practical human. Money for me is more of a necessary abstraction. I can't always do the math. Weighing my unlimited love for the world against my very limited means, I almost always get it wrong.

One time, when I dragged Newman to New York to see a play by Denis Johnson, a writer we both love, we ran out of money. It was the end of the month, so we checked out of our hotel. We waited a day in the streets for one of our paychecks to clear direct deposit so we could travel home.

Still. I believe in flight. Sometimes I think of that as a strength – "What do you plan to do with your one wild and precious life?" my beloved poet Mary Oliver asked.

And still my family is lovely and beckoning.

I am bound to it.

I love Ocean City now because being there with my husband lets me share the parts of his life I missed and wish I didn't. This is the thing about finding love late in life—there is so much that's happened without you, so much to reconstruct, so much to envy, that maybe most of all.

Also, Ocean City Thrasher's fries are amazing. Those seagulls know. Smart birds.

But Paris. And Europe. Mayonnaise on fries. Standing on the Eiffel Tower, looking down on the clouds, tiny planes at your feet.

That's something, too.

Once, when Locklin was maybe six months old and my mother was still alive, she watched him for a weekend while Newman and I went to Ocean City, just the two of us, an escape from the pressures of new parenthood.

This was a huge deal. To be alone, together, two whole days at a beach, seemed like divine intervention.

"Plus we can get a room for 50 bucks," Newman said.

We rented a room in a Victorian B&B for around $40 a night. The room was lovely—purple-flowered wallpaper, a big sturdy wood bed, white rocking chairs on a front porch, a block from the beach.

In that moment, Ocean City was the most beautiful place I'd ever seen.

Back home, Newman and I hadn't had much time alone. Locklin cried a lot. He threw up all the time.

"Some kids are gifted like that," Dr. V, Locklin's pediatrician, said.

Let's talk about puking. Throwing up. Being sick like that. It's one of the things that's terrifying about cancer. It's one of the things I push away and try not to think about.

But about my son: Locklin threw up with gusto.

He threw up when he didn't want to go to bed.

He threw up when he was unhappy.

He threw up when he didn't get his way.

He threw up when he felt we weren't listening to him.

He threw up. Always.

Locklin started speaking at six months. He started with words—light, duck—then moved to sentences—"Light on," "Light off," "Duck!" Everything my son said was a command.

"He's not supposed to do that," a woman at my son's daycare center said to me one day and handed Locklin to me like he was possessed.

"Ah, a gifted puker!" Dr. V, who had kids of his own, who wore Looney Toons ties and had spiky boyish hair and was, mostly, unflappable, said. "It's their way of controlling their world. It will pass. Maybe. Probably."

Newman was working long hours as a bookstore manager. His boss was a monster in expensive pastel pantsuits who believed anyone with a family was just trying to fuck her over. When Newman took two days off for Locklin's birth to be in the delivery room with me, his boss shouted him down for a week, saying, "You took advantage of your wife's pregnancy!"

Newman was so stressed his goatee started to look like he had mange. The cuticles on his right hand oozed green pus.

When people talk about the effects of stress on health, I see gobs of pus the color of glow sticks I squeezed from my husband's fingertips. I see my husband's red chapped hands drenched in peroxide and remember how oddly satisfying it was when the peroxide bubbled and fizzed, the tangible representation of the pain work inflicted on people.

Most mornings Newman woke at 4 A.M. and left by 4:30. He never arrived home before six in the evening. On Saturdays he worked from 6 in the morning until 11 at night, then drove home, and rocked our son to sleep. We'd sit up and talk and eat something, trying to make sense of our life, plotting how we could spend more time with each other and still manage our bills.

This would go on until 2 A.M. Then he'd get up at 4 again.

"I think I'm dying," Newman said one night.

I said, "No, you're not."

Newman said, "This job is fucking killing me."

I said, "I'll save you," and poured more peroxide.

"Light off," Locklin yelled from his crib. "Light on."

The sound of retching.

Ocean City, that working-person's paradise, a tiny joy. Boardwalks. Cheap food. Fun. A chance to be with my husband and take off my clothes. A respite.

Respite.

I've always loved that word.

I was still breastfeeding, but I pumped enough milk to hold my son for the weekend. My mother, the nurse, knew some things about some things.

"We'll be fine," she said, even though she looked worried, maybe because Locklin, so tiny, so sweet-looking when she held him in the doorway and waved goodbye, had the personality of an iceberg and my mother was, more or less, the Titanic.

"Duck!" our son yelled as we drove off.

Newman and I spent a lot of that weekend having sex. I wore lingerie—thigh highs, a bustier. Most of my body, breasts aside, had returned to the body it was before I carried my son, but I felt self-conscious. I sometimes imagined myself forever round, forever bloated, uncomfortable. I often felt disembodied, like who I was had little to do with the physical space I filled up. This is something I never felt before I had children, though later, as I aged, it would resurface ten-fold.

The body I live in isn't a representation of who or what I feel I am, though I don't have the language to express that just yet. *A shell*, spiritual people call physical bodies. I like that, I believe that, though combing the beach it's the glimmering shells I want to save.

It's not that I want to be beautiful, which I do, but that I want to be beautiful and live. For my husband. My kids.

For me. That. It feels small and selfish to say so.

Back in Ocean City, I'd often be on top when Newman and I had sex and when I came, my breasts would spray milk. I was embarrassed at first, drowning my husband's face in milk spray, but he opened his mouth and brought his lips to my nipples and took it in.

All the sex made my breasts fill and hurt more, and so Newman and I fucked more because we loved each other and because sex eased the pressure.

When I came, I felt like a Las Vegas fountain, that cheesy and ridiculous and weird and amazing. It felt like a baptism.

I'm sorry. I can't find other words for this.

Newman and I were married in Vegas, in a little white chapel. We couldn't afford to be married by Elvis the Pelvis, so we hired a $50 generic preacher instead. The preacher's secretary stood in as our witness, which cost another $25. Later, we posed for pictures by Bellagio, the dancing fountains. We posed for pictures by New York, New York. The limo driver who stopped to allow us pictures by every fountain wanted another $50 per stop.

So many fountains.

So much money we didn't have.

Vegas, a desert full of fountains, all those miraged hopes and dreams.

In all the books I read about childbirth and motherhood, none talked about the effect of sex on breast milk, on the size of your tits. It was as if, once a person became a mother and a person became a father, such things were not to be spoken of, ever.

I'm sorry if this offends.

Indulgence. Indulgence. My husband and I were parents and we still wanted sex.

In Ocean City, when Newman and I weren't fucking, which was rare, my breasts would swell and ache and throb and I'd have to squeeze the built-up milk into the sink, which seemed wasteful. Our son wasn't near, but my breasts kept imagining him as needy. I could feel his tears, his hunger, beckoning inside me like a pulse.

We had a schedule, my son and I, and my breasts stuck to it. When I drifted to sleep in my husband's arms, I imagined my son's crying and my breasts would swell into balloons. Leaky balloons. Newman went on sleeping as I leaked. I'd stumble to the bathroom and squirt milk and complain loud enough until my sweet husband woke to help me. He'd squeeze one breast then the other, massaging little circles until the pain eased, the blue-grey milk swirling pretty down the drain. He'd dip in for a sip. He'd dip in and let the milk wash over his face and make all kinds of jokes. He'd sometimes milk one boob, instead of both, then use his other hand to make me come. I loved that. The beauty of transforming pain into love.

But my breasts swelled and leaked at breakfast, and I'd pretend I spilled coffee on my shirt.

My breasts swelled and leaked at the Irish pub we loved, but it was dark in there.

My breasts swelled and leaked at the beach until I worried about sharks and breast milk, breast milk vs. blood in the water and so on.

On the plus side, I think I may have looked okay in a bathing suit then, with my huge milky boobs, the veins pressing up beneath the pale skin, though I would never have believed that. I have a huge ass. My thighs are a mountain range. Crippled as a baby, I don't have calves. I never had boobs until I had my son.

It's a weird and helpless and miraculous thing to have your body morph like that. I felt like an alien. I felt like Venus, those sculptures by Rodin, but come to life, the veins pulsing, my skin pulled translucent from the pressure, those veins, a map straight to my heart. *Vena amoris.*

I tried not to be embarrassed by it all. Then I felt like a god. Both. Neither.

Why didn't any of those *What to Expect* books I read mention that?

What is the word in *Words With Friends* that could hold all of this? A word like that would be worth so many points. A bingo for sure.

In Ocean City, Polish Water Ice is a treat for the whole family. There's a loudspeaker that broadcasts that message all along the boardwalk.

Polish Water Ice is like Italian Ice, but cheaper. Creamier, maybe.

My father was Polish. I know a few phrases.

Boże pomóż mi. God help me.

Boże, pomóż nam wszystkim. God help us all.

Co cialo lubi, to dusze zgubi.

What likes the body will lose the soul.

A shell. A shell.

In Ocean City, you get a free hermit crab with the purchase of a cage.

I sometimes think about my Hooters friend, Miss February. I wonder where she is, if she's still alive and gorgeous as always, if she has kids, if she found love, if she's still flying. I wonder how her lovely boobs have held up through the years, if she kept her Hooters uniform in a closet, if she ever looks at it and thinks what the hell.

She had the loveliest blue eyes. I forgot that until just now.

Once, when we were on a layover in Madrid, she pulled a ragged copy of *A Moveable Feast* out of her flight bag and we talked about our love of Hemingway and how when we were in high school we both thought that book was a map of the world we wanted to see.

And we did. We saw it.

Life delights in life, William Blake said.

To live is so startling, Emily Dickinson said.

Miss February. My beautiful friend.

If you read this, let me know how you're doing.

Adult Mart

Chapter 12

Somewhere between the time our son was born and the time Newman and I went to Ocean City alone, the three of us drove to Adult Mart in Monroeville. Newman and I were determined to keep our sex life alive, even though our son was months old, maybe because our son was months old.

Adult Mart is a sweet place, staffed by women who are happy to put fresh batteries into a vibrator and let customers feel the vibration against their palms. They never mock anyone for buying leopard-fur handcuffs or an inflatable doll out of loneliness or horniness or both. They never ask questions. Bless them. Adult Mart is designed to keep love alive, wherever and however you find it.

Adult Mart is located across the street from a graveyard and a strip mall called Miracle Mile. The graveyard reminds shoppers of our own mortality by marking death with headstones built to outlast us all. Miracle Mile is designed to be a miracle, a place where people flock for office supplies and candles and shoes and believe that everything that can be bought will save us. Miracle Mile features a Five Below, a store where everything costs $5 and below, and where everything you buy breaks within five minutes unless you buy candy, which is stale and overpriced.

Miracle Mile in Monroeville, Pennsylvania, is a capitalist's dream.

Next door to Adult Mart is a bank and a Petco, the place to go for provisions for emotional-support animals, or to adopt an emotional-support animal, a ferret maybe, or a pedigree dog you can buy on an installment plan. Some days the block where Adult Mart stands looks like one big metaphor, a map of the human condition. Sex and death. Commerce and commodity. The search for companionship and unconditional love and reasonably priced vibrators. A mile filled with miracles and broken Bluetooth speakers.

On the day in question, Newman went into Adult Mart to buy me lingerie and one of those vibrators. He cares about me, always. I didn't know much about vibrators. He assured me they were great.

I stayed in the parking lot with our baby son. We parked next door, in the bank parking lot so I wouldn't feel gross. I sometimes feel gross, not because I'm judging anyone, except I judge myself. Blame my parents, who I love dearly. Blame Catholic guilt. Blame those *What to Expect* books and parenting magazines and everything that says, implicitly or explicitly, that motherhood requires erasure of the self. But I'm getting preachy.

Newman jumped over the guardrail like the athlete he was before I knew him.

Locklin was in his car seat. I watched my husband, still graceful, still horny, making a bee-line for Adult Mart, that beacon of love and hope. And then Locklin started crying. Louder. Louder. He made sounds like he was trying to puke.

"Aw, a gifted puker!" Dr. V, who would not have approved of Adult Mart with a baby in the car, would say.

I climbed in the backseat.

I unbuckled my son and pulled him to me.

I lifted my shirt and breastfed him, which is what I did whenever my son cried, which is what I did despite what Dr. V said, which is "Don't let him feed on you," as if my son were a vampire or zombie, something to fear.

Maybe I did fear my son a little. I feared his crying. I feared his sadness. I feared the puking.

I wanted the world to be gentle for him and I wanted to show him gentle. And so, I held my son to my breast and rocked him and felt as I always did, which is as if we were alone in the world, the two of us, but of course we weren't.

Without me noticing, another car had pulled into the Adult Mart parking lot, a middle-aged man in a white BMW. His car faced our car in the bank parking lot, the guardrail between us. The man in the white BMW was staring at our car, which was rusty, an old Ford, and I couldn't tell how much he could see or how much he couldn't. I was so embarrassed I put my head down. I caught the shimmer of his car-door handles. They were gold-colored and glinted in the sun. They may have been real gold for all I knew.

I didn't understand anything anymore.

By the time Newman came back with a bubblegum-pink bag filled with fishnet lingerie and a vibrator shaped like a butterfly, I was weeping, something he'd never seen me do. I didn't know if I was crying because the rich man with the comb-over was leering at my son and me, or if I was crying because the world I'd known wasn't the world anymore and I hadn't figured out how to blend these worlds.

I felt dirty, guilty, an un-mother. A woman in a rusty Ford who couldn't afford a decent car, let alone tinted windows.

That.

Locklin went on sucking, happy, quiet, content.

"What's wrong?" Newman asked, and I couldn't say anything.

I've never told anyone this story until now.

Something about a crisis brings out things in people. A need to talk things through, a need to remember and mark moments that say I was here, and here, and here.

"You feel me?" kids say these days.

You feel me?

The fear of being a bad mother, selfish, worse. It's probably something most mothers feel, but maybe some more than others.

I mentioned I'm adopted, with no medical history beyond hearsay.

"I would have aborted you if I could," my birth mother wrote to me in email, and then again on social media, like we were fighting teenagers. She told me who my birth father was on social media, a DM. "He will deny you," she wrote. "There is no denying!"

I understand my birth mother's unresolved shame, but to have anyone wish you dead hurts.

Who tells a person who their father is on the fucking internet?

My mother is the mother who raised me and loved me.

My father is the father who raised me and loved me.

And still.

Adopted people, when we talk about our families, our origins, sound crazy at best. We work to find language: the parents who raised me, birth mother, birth father, half-sibling, sort-of sister, bio-brother, etc.

Neither of my parents, the parents who raised me, would have ever wished me dead. The opposite, of course.

My parents raised me to believe that no one would wish me dead because I held value as a person. I was a gift. Their gift. Chosen, whatever.

I am lucky to have been raised like that. Lucky life.

I'd like to say I wish my birth mother well, but I'd be lying.

Sometimes I imagine my birth mother's breasts, what happened to them after she gave me up. How much they must have hurt. How they must have leaked and throbbed.

I wonder how well the medications the doctors gave her to dry them up worked, how well they erased any trace of me.

If she thought of me, ever. That.

I wonder if she ever had to squeeze milk into a sink and how awful that might have been for her. Or what a relief it might have been for her. Both. Or erotic.

She had four children after me. I don't know if she breastfed them, but it's a question maybe.

The nurse at the hospital when I was there with my son wished for me to eat something so I could go on providing, the love of a mother for her child a given even so.

My breasts in Ocean City swelled and ached and spewed.

My breasts in the Adult Mart parking lot swelled and ached.

Every time my son cried, I felt it in my spine, a searing pain. Every time my children cry or cough or sigh now, I feel it in my spine, my cells, my blood. It's a visceral thing, but maybe not for all mothers. Maybe it's visceral only if you're open and have space for it.

"You do you," people say now and call it self-care.

But when you do you, someone else has to pick up the detritus. Who mops up all the residual mess?

What do you do when someone wishes you dead on a computer? When someone wishes you dead, what do you wish for them?

What can I wish for my birth mother that's not awful?

"Forgive us our trespasses," the Catholic in me can't shake, "as we forgive those who trespass against us."

The doctors who ordered my biopsy ordered genetic testing, too. I'm not sure if genetic test results will make me feel better or worse, but I want them for my children's sake, so they can prepare for what their wiring insists.

It's terrible not to know things.

It's terrible to know things, too.

Nature. Nurture. Cancer is in my genetics, but not something I must pass to my children.

The science will tell me we're clear.

Clear.

I will always be my parents' child, the ones who raised me, the ones who died of cancer.

Andy Warhola Meets the Breatharians

Chapter 13

As for cancer-killing diets, model Valeria Lukyanova, Internet-famous as The Human Barbie, says Breatharian is best.

For a while, Valeria Lukyanova—5'7" and 100 pounds with a thimble waist and fake boobs the size of clown cars—stopped eating. She stopped drinking water. Valeria Lukyanova says she can live on air and sunshine. She calls air and sunshine *cosmic micro-food.* She says anything else is poison.

Valeria Lukyanova, an instructor at the School of Out-of-Body Travel, says she's from another planet and speaks to her fellow aliens through the light she eats. Valeria Lukyanova is a racist and a lunatic, but—should her diet work—I would try her diet.

But I am mostly sane, so I have not considered Breatharianism.

I get updates on Pittsburgh's air quality on an app on my phone. Bad-air-day emojis are smiley faces covered with surgical masks, or smiley faces coughing smog.

A while back, a Google employee, a transplant from San Francisco to Pittsburgh, wrote an op-ed wailing about how rotten Pittsburgh air is. He couldn't sleep. He couldn't go outside. Even his dog was wheezing. He couldn't imagine how anyone lived here. Pittsburgh might as well be Mars, unfit for human life.

"That's it. I'm done," he wrote.

He said he was moving to Portland.

I and nearly every local-born Pittsburgher I know mocked this guy. We said good riddance, bye-bye now, don't let the door hit you in the ass, etc.

Pittsburghers have a general disdain for entitled rich people who move here from places like Brooklyn or San Francisco. They've driven housing prices up. They've brought in artisanal toast and duck speck. These strangers mock Pittsburgh accents. They turn the sites of mills into luxury condos and call them historic, quaint.

"Pussy," I and people I know said about the Google guy.

A personal history of Pittsburgh air quality:

As a kid, when I'd blow my nose, the Kleenex would turn black.

My father, who built our house, worked in a mill that specialized in graphite.

He carried a handkerchief, a hanky, in his pocket and it was always black and crusty.

My father's skin was grey, no matter how much he scrubbed. He'd try to get his hands clean with bleach. He'd try to get his hands clean with Brillo Pads.

Andy Warhol made Brillo Pads famous in his paintings. Andy Warhol said everyone would be famous for 15 minutes.

Sometimes I Google my father's name, hoping I will find him. My father was never famous, though he should have been. His name appears in the 1940 U.S. Census, the Death Index, and World War II Draft Cards. His obituary comes up, too.

There is no mention of my father's singing voice, not even in the obituary. I should have written my father's obituary, but back then, the funeral director handled that. Everything standard, everything on a form, death as ordinary as applying for a library card.

How did you calculate those 15 minutes, Andy Warhol?

One of my first jobs was working the obituary desk at a daily newspaper. To spell someone's name wrong in an obituary is one of the worst things anyone can do as a journalist. Sometimes an obituary is the only time a person's family will ever see their loved one's name in print. Sometimes an obituary is the only evidence a person has ever been alive.

Consider the weight of that.

I was 19 years old, working at *The Erie Daily Times* in Erie, Pennsylvania, terrorized by an editor named Phyllis. Phyllis wore beige suits with shoulder pads that could double as toasters, and thick round-framed glasses that made her eyes bulge like her thyroid was about to explode. Phyllis circled the newsroom like a shark and reminded everyone she used to work at *Newsday* in New York City.

"A real newspaper, in a real city," Phyllis would say.

How Phyllis ended up in Erie, Pennsylvania—a place where snowfall is measured in feet and not inches, a place where, during high tide, dead fish wash up on roadways and are left there to molder in whatever sun dares show up—was never clear, and no one dared ask.

When Phyllis was angry, and Phyllis was always angry, her eyes turned blowfish. Her New York accent was a switchblade and she'd wield a lit cigarette as if, at any moment, she'd planned to put it out on someone's face.

Her favorite word was crap.

As in, "Don't give me that crap," and "What is this crap?" and "Stop crapping around, you crap-asses," and "Deadline, crap-tards."

I'd spend nights lying awake, staring at the water stain on my college-apartment ceiling, considering the stain an ink-blot, imagining Phyllis's owl face hovering over me as I worried over the spellings of the names of the dead.

This was many years ago, of course.

Phyllis is, I'm sure, among the dead now.

I hope whoever filled out her obituary form got it right.

I hope it said she used to work at *Newsday.*

I wish there were a place in her obituary for the word crap because Phyllis would have liked that.

"We're in the truth business," Phyllis liked to say.

Truth = anti-crap.

The plain truth. The plain.

I learned a lot from Phyllis, terror aside.

Maybe Andy Warhol never considered an obituary when he imagined those 15 minutes of fame. Or maybe that's what he meant.

Maybe Andy Warhol thought a life was worth less if it didn't happen in front of a camera, if it didn't make the news.

Mark this: Andy Warhola was from Pittsburgh, Pennsylvania. He's buried here, too, next to his parents Julia and Andrej Warhola, at St. John the Baptist Byzantine Catholic Cemetery in Pittsburgh, Pennsylvania.

"I never understood why when you died, you didn't just vanish, and everything could just keep going on the way it was only you just wouldn't be there," Andy said. "I always thought I'd like my own tombstone to be blank. No epitaph and no name. Well, actually, I'd like it to say 'figment.'"

Andy Warhol's grave site is viewable 24 hours a day, seven days a week through a collaborative project between The Warhol Museum and EarthCam. The project is called Figment. A webcam records everything that's happened at Andy's gravesite since his death and so on. His tombstone says Andy Warhol. His birth date: August 6, 1928. His death: February 22, 1987.

I once set a can of soup on his grave.

Those Brillo Pads Andy made famous are steel wool. People leave those at his grave, too.

Pittsburgh's steelworkers like my father used steel wool to scrub steel from their bodies. Circle of life.

Andy Warhol's hands were soft and smooth.

The Brillo Pad website claims the word brillo is Latin for "bright," though there is no such Latin word. It's all marketing. Corinthian Leather from New Jersey. Lynyrd Skynyrd. All those Ys.

"Happy crap," Phyllis the editor would say.

I'd pluck metal shards from my father's face and palms with tweezers. I loved to do this, the way I still love to pop pimples and beg my teenage kids to give me their faces and backs to work on. Sometimes it was hard to tell which shards in my father's skin came from Brillo Pads and which from the mill. My father would joke about how he could set off metal detectors at the airport if he could ever get a vacation.

"If I could just get away," my father would say when he was well, then when he was sick, as if a change of scenery would cure him of cancer.

Isn't that what we're talking about? How we'd all like to find a place, a respite, somewhere we could rest a while and live. Just live.

My cancer. I want to make too much of it. I want to make it a joke. Knock knock.

I'd like to see Paris again.

On their last trip together, my father and mother were in a car, heading for Las Vegas, my father's favorite place, the magic of water in the desert, lucky at last. On the way to the airport, my mother said my father was driving erratically, weaving lanes, no turn signal.

Even on a good day, my father didn't believe in turn signals. "The bastards think I'm going to waste a bulb on them?" he'd say about other drivers.

A turn-signal bulb costs maybe $1.50.

War does things to people. So does working in a mill. My father was not Kurt Vonnegut. For my father, World War II broke his belief in humanity.

"Be kind, babies," Kurt Vonnegut, who survived the bombing of Dresden, advised other humans, his advice for going on living.

"Fuck them all," my father said about the people on the road who needed to know when or if he was going to turn.

Fuck those people who thought my father wasn't strong enough to live forever. Fuck those people who did unspeakable things to other people.

"I thought he was going to kill us," my mother said later, but I'm sure in the car she said nothing. I'm sure my mother pressed her foot to the floor mat on her side, where the brake would be if she were driving. The mat there was worn down, a hole through the carpet.

Throughout their 50 years of marriage, my father always drove. My mother was always the passenger.

My mother wasn't weak. She knew it mattered to my father that he was the one driving and she let him drive, even if her life depended on it.

Love is like that, maybe. Maybe we all give over parts of ourselves and the parts we give over make us more beautiful. Or maybe I'm just prettifying things.

And so it goes. Dear Vonnegut.

Halfway to the airport, my father realized he forgot his wallet. They had to turn back. My father motherfucked everyone, including my mother, the president, his doctors, PennDOT, all the way home.

My parents missed their flight. A blessing, my mother called it later.

"God was with us," my mother said, prettifying, though she rarely went to church and when she did, she didn't listen to a word the priest said because she said the priest was full of crap.

Bless you, Phyllis, full of grace. May your favorite word *crap* live on and on.

My mother convinced my father to go to the doctor, who did some tests, lung X-ray, brain scan, MRI.

"How old are you?" the doctor, who read cancer like a map, asked my father.

My father answered.

"Well, you've lived your life," the doctor said when he told my father the cancer had moved to his brain. The insult of that.

I've written this over and over because the insult mattered so much to my father.

It mattered, and goes on mattering so much to me. It's what I aspire not to be, a person who denigrates someone for their life.

"In order to write about life, you first must live it," Hemingway said.

"What will you do with your one wild and precious life?" Mary Oliver wrote.

"Well, you've lived your life," the doctor said to my father.

Imagine someone saying that to you.

Imagine someone saying that to anyone you love.

Go Beyond the Pain

Chapter 14

My surgery is soon and I'm miserable and stressed. My surgery—double mastectomy, reconstruction using my own tissue, which means stomach fat, microscopic surgery, something called DIEP, pronounced deep, two brilliant Pittsburgh surgeons, 13 hours under, a miracle, seriously.

Still.

Things that shouldn't hurt, things not diagnosed, hurt. My hands. My shoulders. Every inch of my body, this shell, throbs.

I wake up this morning hobbled, like someone beat my legs with a broom all night. I limp to the kitchen the way my mother and father did when they were alive and only a little older than I am now.

"You don't know how much it hurts me," my mother said, and she meant arthritis, but I think she meant living.

What's wrong with me now—cancer, whatever—is not so bad, I think, but still, we're getting there. I could die.

So could you.

I will. You will.

Temporary. Temporary.

I get some iced tea from the fridge and drink it straight from the carton and feel guilty for how often I blame my kids for that.

Be civilized. Get a glass already.

Back in bed, I wrap my legs over my husband's legs. Newman's slept in his socks again.

"Cold feet, warm heart," the old wives said.

Who were these old wives? And where did they glean all that wisdom?

I flop and try to wake my husband.

I don't know why, but lately I resent that my husband sleeps. I want him to be awake and ready, always.

I love you Newman. Stay awake and help me.

I keep flopping. I flop again. I want my husband to notice my flops.

Maybe he wants to sneak sex in before the alarms rattle, the texts and emails vibrate, all that electric shock of this world. I also want an audience, someone to complain to about my legs, my body, mortality, all these aches, whatever, a jerk thing to do, but still.

I am by nature a complainer, though I fight against it. Complainers complain no matter where or why, serious or not.

This is serious. I will likely live through it. Temporary.

Temporary.

I am an old wife now.

Sorry again about that iced tea.

///

I stroke my husband's face, brush my thumb over his eyebrows, make the hairs stand up straight, like the eyebrows of a madman who must wear socks with rubber pads on the soles to keep his cold feet from sliding around the psych ward.

I have cancer. Cancer. Jesus, that word.

I am that and not that.

I am that and rejecting it.

My mind is filled with so much darkness, so many fears for my husband and children, so I work at my prayers. I repeat my favorite lines from my favorite poems, my favorite poets, those prophets, my beloveds even so.

"Stand up for the stupid and the crazy," the Whitman my husband and I both love said.

And the old. And the sick. And the lonely. And the frightened.

I am frightened, not of dying but of everyone I love dying and leaving me alone.

And the lost. And the unloved. And the abandoned. And the forgotten.

I'm sick, whatever, but what I fear more—being forgotten. What I fear more—my husband will die in his sleep. I keep one hand on him all night and feel his chest rise and fall while he lies oblivious in his own peaceable kingdom. When my children were young, I'd do this to them, too, remember? One hand in a crib, reaching up through the bars to count the breaths with my fingers, a musician learning keys.

I did this for my father when he was dying. I did this for my mother when she was dying. I know my mother did this to me, too, and I swore I would be less fearful, that I wouldn't give my courage away, but we become everything we said we would not become and, in the end, that's mostly okay.

I did my best. Everyone I loved did their best.

"I'm sorry," my mother said when she was dying. "I'm sorry I wasn't a better mother. I'm sorry I was nervous all the time."

And the nervous.

And the heartbroken.

And the remorseful.

I don't know if my husband reaches over to feel my breathing at night.

I don't know what he fears.

I snore a lot and sometimes my husband shoves me awake, gentle-like, and I roll over so he can get a little rest before work.

One time, when I'd quit wearing my mouthpiece which was supposed to stop me from snoring but which never stopped me from snoring, my husband shoved me awake. I said I wasn't snoring at all, that he was the one snoring, but he recorded me—seriously, who does that?—and my own snoring sounded like a cartoon, Elmer Fudd, maybe.

If you don't know Elmer Fudd or Bugs Bunny, I'm sorry. They're from the 1900s. Look it up, you beauties.

My husband and I have been married a long time, twenty years plus now.

"I know this defies the laws of gravity," Bugs told Elmer Fudd. "But I ain't never studied law."

In cartoons you can get shot in the face for a laugh and keep coming back and back.

I'd like a body like that, one that goes on, one that heals itself to keep making jokes. Road Runner. Bugs. Elmer Fudd. Immortal.

I take a lot of Aleve.

Go beyond the pain, the Aleve commercials say.

Still, I'm grateful for everything I feel—my husband's skin on my skin, our lumpy bed, each side worn down to the shape of our thick middle-aged bodies, the gravity of that, and how we can lie there and talk before drifting off—about Whitman and books and our dreams and how amazing to still have dreams at our age.

On our sixteenth anniversary I joked we'd earned our licenses to drive away, throw every hard thing into the rearview, and wave each other on to our next lives.

But we want to be here, together, holding on, 20 years, steady as she goes.

Grace Paley said about aging and mortality, "When you get up every morning, you must take your heart in your two hands."

I take my husband's sweet sleeping face in my two hands and smooth his wacky eyebrows.

"The future is no more uncertain than the present," our dear Whitman says.

What I know this morning: the world will go on a little while longer. And we will go on with it.

The blessed shipwrecked beauty of that.

Tommy Lee's Penis and Me

Epilogue 1

Lately I've been thinking a lot about Tommy Lee's penis.

I haven't been to a Mötley Crüe concert in years, unless you count the Mötley Crüe cover band that played Club 80's in my hometown, Trafford, Pennsylvania, a few months back.

The cover band was pretty good, even if Nikki Sixx's facial hair was sketched on with a Sharpie and the pyro was just glitter lights and one of the Nasty Habits was a 50-something sweetheart who knew my husband from working a latchkey program for kids back in the 1990s.

I wasn't much of a hair-metal fan despite growing up in the 1980s. But it's 2023 now, and Tommy Lee's persistence about pulling his junk out—at concerts; on Instagram; on Only Fans, where people pony up money to see Tommy Lee's penis even though they can Google it for free—that has me pondering things.

Tommy Lee is 59, just a year older than I am now.

Maybe it's about mortality, something beyond a mid-life crisis, something more urgent, more desperate, because let's face it, neither I nor Tommy Lee are living to be even close to 118 years old.

"The older I get, the more I don't care what people think or what people say," Tommy Lee says. "I just do what moves me."

Maybe showing the world his penis moves Tommy Lee.

Maybe flashing his junk is what makes Tommy Lee feel most alive.

Or maybe Tommy Lee is simply a rich idiot, a penis-narcissist who can play drums upside down and has the word *Mayhem* tattooed on his torso.

But like most things I think about, this isn't about that.

Tommy Lee's penis, which had a speaking role and was both animatronic and a puppet in the Hulu series *Pam & Tommy*, makes me think about other things.

Boobs, mostly.

Tits. Breasts. Ta-tas. Mine.

Before Tommy Lee started pulling it all out at Mötley Crüe shows and encouraging men in the audience to do likewise, which seems scary, it was mostly women flashing their lovely tits.

When we saw Mötley Crüe years ago in Cleveland, Newman tried to get me to be a good sport, flash my tits, get in on the fun. Newman, as I've probably made clear, is adorable, with these gem-blue eyes and almost-cherubic rosy cheeks and a goatee that makes him look like an extra on *Sons of Anarchy*.

He is completely devastatingly dangerously charming.

Whatever, Newman.

I didn't do it.

Back then, my boobs, tits, breasts were, as far as I knew, cancer-free. They were completely my own. Still, I would have rather shown strangers the balance in my bank account than show them what I think might have been fine and perfectly hair-metal-acceptable tits. I would have rather let strangers wriggle around in my underwear drawer or read my teenage diary or clean my toilet than let them see even a snippet of authentic nipple.

Flash forward a few years. Cancer, cancer. You know the story. A double mastectomy. DIEP tissue reconstruction. Breasts, tits, boobs that are mine but not mine.

Surgeons, artists really, sculpted my body back into something non-lethal, something so closely resembling my former body, but better than my former body, that I must look close to map the scars and make sure I didn't imagine everything.

And now I want to show everyone, as if my boobs are not my body, as if they are evidence, maybe–proof that something tried to kill me and missed.

One time, a friend in New York was shot when he was stopped at a red light in Newark. The doctors left the bullet in his body because it would be more dangerous to try to remove it.

"You can feel it," he'd say to anyone he told his story to—strangers in bars or on airplanes or at parties. He'd lift his shirt and take the person's hand and place it where the bullet lodged near his left shoulder, just above his heart.

"Isn't that some shit?" my friend would say. He'd shake his head no, as if even years later, he couldn't believe his luck.

The bullet beneath his skin felt like what it was—hard, foreign, but so small, considering. The scar looked like a tiny sun, almost pretty.

These tits that aren't my own are lovely in their way, too.

"Foobs," my fellow DIEP sisters call them. Fake, but not fake. So real-seeming, so death-defying, so prone to gravity they sag, whatever.

Thank you, Dr. Gimble. Thank you, Dr. Johnson. Thank you, dear Pittsburgh, with your world-class hospitals dotting our skyline like stars.

Also, the thing with DIEP reconstruction—which is micro-surgery that uses your own tissue, say belly or thigh fat, rather than implants to make boobs where boobs used to be—is that you lose feeling.

In other words, a creep on the subway could grope my boobs and I wouldn't feel a thing. This is not an invitation, creep on the subway.

I am, as Pink Floyd would say, comfortably numb.

"Belly-titsasauras," my daughter Phelan likes to tease, like I'm something that should be extinct but isn't.

"Do your boobs growl when you get hungry?" she wants to know, since my boobs came straight from my stomach, right around the spot where Tommy Lee has that Mayhem tattoo.

This is all disembodied, maybe. Which might be what Tommy Lee feels—disembodied. A disconnection between who he is as a human and who he is as a rock star with tattoos that probably cost more than I've made in a lifetime.

Tommy Lee's full-frontal on Instagram appeared between two other photos—one of a banana, and another of an elephant standing face-to-face with a naked guy.

The elephant asks the naked guy, "How do you breathe through that little thing?"

The penis in *Pam & Tommy*, according to *Variety*, was voiced by comic Jason Mantzoukas, who is voice-famous for shows like *Big Mouth* and *Star Trek: Prodigy*.

The penis in *Pam & Tommy* was controlled by four puppeteers.

"Four puppeteers!" the elephant in Tommy Lee's Instagram post might say. "Niiiiiiiice."

What I'm saying is, I've shown a lot of people my boobs, tits, breasts, whatever. I've whipped them out at parties. I've let many people touch them. I've lost count.

Chances are, if you ask me, I'll show them to you, too. Because life is so precious and fleeting.

Proof of life.

Still here. Still here.

Epilogue 2

This book has been a time capsule of an ordinary life. The root of *ordinary* is Latin, of course, and French, too. *Orderly.*

"Not that it was beautiful," the poet Anne Sexton wrote, "but that, in the end, there was a certain sense of order there; something worth learning in that narrow diary of my mind."

This has been a book about cancer. Cancer-ish. A diagnosis. Mine. Other people's. I had some surgeries and doctors did some things. The first surgery was 13 hours, the best sleep of my life. You get near death, you don't think about death. You think about sleep, maybe, and how tired you are. It never occurred to me I might not wake up.

What I thought:

My son. My daughter. My husband.

The sweet anesthesiologists played "Comfortably Numb," by Pink Floyd. The anesthesiologists were so handsome, so sweet. They waved to me as I drifted off. Buh-bye now.

I trusted them. They were lovely companions, funny, steady. I would trust them to carry me over into whatever life is after this one and so on.

"Bellytits-asauraus. Do your boobs growl when you're hungry?" my daughter says over and over. It's a great joke and I don't get tired of it.

I am alive for now. Not extinct. I am grateful and hungry. Hungry for more time, more of this world before whatever comes after.

The details of that, beyond what I've written here, seem small.

We're here. We're born and live a while, the Spider said in *Charlotte's Web.*

Dear E.B. White.

We get to love one another in this life.

How amazing is that?

We live. We die.

Okay. I love you. Even so.

In Gratitude

Endless thanks to my children—Locklin and Phelan Newman—my hearts who endure having two writer-parents, sweet Jesus, and who have their own magical lives and stories to tell. May your lives be so full that your stories are endless. I love you so much. Thank you to editor and publisher Dan Cafaro, whose enduring love for writers and writing keeps hope alive. You are our Sylvia Beach. Thank you for believing in this weird little book. Thank you to my forever-beloveds, near and not-so-near—most especially Sylvia Catello, my sweet soul sister—your friendship is magic and means way more than blood to me. I love you so much. And thank you to all my Catellos—you beauties; and to Conrad and Juliet; Lou Ickes; Carol Agostinelli Bachman; Tammy Knopf; Carrie Wagner; Trish Reinhold Masley; Becky Jung; Anita Rometo; Sinead Lawless; Meghan and Abbie; Scott Silsbe; Bob and Amy; J.B.; TT Kapis; and so many more. Your friendships hold me to this world. I hope I can anchor you back. Thank you to my doctors, Dr. Ron Johnson and Dr. Michael Gimbel, for rebuilding me. You're brilliant and funny and sweet and you probably have no idea how much that means, especially the funny. Thank you to Pittsburgh and New York, my city loves. Thank you to Pitt-Greensburg and my sweet students. You keep me going and going. Thank you to my parents, Bertie and Walt Jakiela. I wish you were here. And thank you to Newman, always, all ways. We've had a lot of good years and years to go.

About the Author

Lori Jakiela is the author of seven books, including the award-winning memoir, *Belief Is Its Own Kind of Truth, Maybe* (Atticus Books, 2015). Her work has appeared in *The New York Times, The Washington Post, The Chicago Tribune*, and many other places. She is currently a professor of English/Creative Writing at The University of Pittsburgh at Greensburg, where she directs the Creative & Professional Writing Program. A former international flight attendant, she lives in her hometown, Trafford, Pa., with her husband, the author Dave Newman, and their children.